Federico Sargentone
MIDCAREER WRITING

Federico Sargentone
Midcareer Writing
Sorry Press®, Munich 2025
Editing: Lukas Kubina
Design: Wiegand von Hartmann
Printing: KOPA

Cover Image:
Philip-Lorca diCorcia, *Head #10* (2000)
Image courtesy of Sprüth Magers,
Berlin; London; Los Angeles; New York.

Thanks to Carlotta Maneschi for precious,
additional editorial coordination in close relationship
with the author.

Thanks to Jacob Wise for the use of a
mid-progress version of serif typeface Gablet.

Printed in Lithuania
ISBN 978-3-910265-22-6

Sorry Press®
Theresienstr. 16
80333 Munich, Germany
info@sorry-press.com

Index

MIDCAREER (INTRO)

It's nothing until it's something. I've been buried in books since I can remember, and I still am. Sometimes in my writing this persona comes up too much, so in this book I decided to leave the "tscholarly" attitude behind. Of course, this is a collection of essays, and that it should be, but in its form, I've tried to inject as much personality and livelihood as I could. The book is, structurally, arranged as a mixtape: there's an intro, an outro, a skit, a freestyle, and an interlude, all punctuated by what the audience will see as singles, bangers, or fillers. Actually: no fillers, but I will wait for the reviews.

This book is about my practice, which I've crafted and steered towards my north star since day one, even though I didn't know it back then. It all makes sense now. I have tried to develop a style of criticism that, since the beginning of my career 10 years ago, combined opinion with critical thinking, oscillating the focus of analysis from highbrow manifestations of culture to niche subcultural phenomena, and back.

As someone who identifies as a writer, when asked, I see myself filling positions that sometimes adhere to the adjacent fields of creative direction, consulting, strategy, and everything in between. This book is a testament to the joy of putting together a thesis, sometimes an antithesis, an opinion, and a conclusion. A testament to the joy of coming up with ideas. Today, finding yourself identifying as a cultural critic is a precious condition. There's more to it. Today. And I hope this book will let people discover that.

This book is about the contemporary state of the world. It is analyzed through the lens of art, music, finance, real estate, literature, rap, drugs, addictions, fashion, and more. In all this, I am an observer, and sometimes a witness or a participant—but never the main character. I have tried to weave my sentiment and opinion within a broader cultural analysis to produce something that's as digestible as it is insightful for different readers and contexts.

I am extremely thankful for anyone who stood by my side in this journey: first and foremost the editors and publishers who gave me a chance throughout my career—an Italian who writes in English, touching on difficult and complex topics—and pushed my writing to wider audiences. Then, I want to thank my partner, my family, and my closest friends for bearing with me—a writer—a schizophrenic, insomniac, neurotic, addictive, fucking, personality. I want to thank the legend Philip-Lorca diCorcia, an icon who has pioneered the art–mass divide way before anyone else, and his gallery Sprüth Magers for letting me use his amazing work on the cover. Lastly, I wish to thank my publishers—Lukas Kubina and Moritz Wiegand—for trusting me with this thing.

This book is printed in extremely large type—this is an actualization of an inherent fear of mine: that of not being read. I apply this thinking to anything I do: if it's not formally big type, it's big words and cheeky statements in writing that, make people disagree, or at least think. The extreme-sized typography in it, for me, reflects my desire for this book to be read by a wide demographic—the same demographic I come from and write for. I believe reading is a synonym for power, and in the book we'll talk about that.

Thank you for reading my book.

GENERATIONAL MYTHOLOGY

We call a generation "all the people of about the same age within a society or within a particular family." And this means that a set of humans living around the same period of time are destined to share behavioral and aesthetic attitudes as if they were all siblings of the same mother-identity. A progeny of ideas, time-space coordinates, and ethics, a new generational cohort is procreated roughly every 15 years; every time a previous generation enrolls in high school, a new one is born and bred from the same source: society.

The process of generational value creation, in which a set of coded characteristics is produced, shared, and validated within the generational identity, is double-edged. On one side, it reflects the internal identity of the generation, and on the other, it mythologizes the external perception of itself. This internal–external process creates values that inform the generation (internally) and project its image beyond itself, into the world (externally). To put it simply—and please excuse any gross generalizations for lack of better theorization strategy only—a generation incubates values that rely on collective adoption, spanning from politics, activism, and ethical conscience to aesthetic tastes in music, fashion, art, and culture at large, that truly inform their internal identity; at the same time, these values are translated into ideas and aesthetic formations that depict the generational image out there, externally.

A straightforward exemplification of the generational value creation process, again generalizing, can be found in the quest for authenticity that informs the generation that is currently under the constant scrutiny of the present: Generation Z. The internal value creation of this particular generation relies on authenticity and related set of behaviors such as political action, ecological awareness, and a strong sense of civic ethics. These internal drivers, among others, shape up the generational conscience, while also being translated into external factors that form the generational image. In the world, we see these drivers reflected in lifestyle choices, aesthetic trends, and style languages that contribute to the mythology of supposedly anyone born between 1996 and 2012.

Within a generation, the creation of internal values translates fluidly into external aesthetic values. The sum of these two is what we could define as the "generational mythology." Every member of this expanded social family contributes a fraction of knowledge, attitude, or sensibility that, via agglomeration with others, constructs the above-mentioned generational identity.

The inherent question that remains unanswered revolves around the ownership of those generational values. Put simply: Who influences, or steers, the wheel of the generational value creation? Who, among all the family members, fuels their set of values to the point they become ideals? And who, among all the faces, is the poster human of their own generation? Obviously, the youth. Or rather, those who enroll when previous generation members graduate. Those who reclaim culture from their predecessors. **THOSE WHO COME OF AGE WHEN THEIR ANTECEDENTS GO OFF AGE.**

A generational mythology is composed of scattered artifacts—material and immaterial—that are collected among the youth and projected into the world. It's a signification process, by which the generation affirms itself from a virtual and actual standpoint. A generational mythology could take many forms, can draw inspiration from many sources, can verify many different attitudes, motifs, and drivers, and its formation process can strongly differ from generation to generation. Think about millennials, and how their strongest fabrication of the "hipster" referenced bohemian codes of conduct, mixed with late-'60s countercultural tropes, and cultural symbology that preceded the generation itself in time. Differently, Gen Z appropriates aesthetic motifs and stylistic languages that were formed and in use during their generational age gap. Y2K, for example, actually happened within the Gen Z cohort, while the "hipster," referenced eras way before the millennial cohort.

The fact that a mythology can be built through a different methodology for each generation doesn't mean that it can't be visualized and marketed. On the contrary, in recent cultural history, the youth, and its symbolism, have been investigated and fetishized with great emphasis. The youth, or the mythology of the youth—whatever their generation—has become a currency traded on the creative global markets, and turned into profit from the cultural stock exchange.

Beatlemania-cum-Swinging London, ushered into 1977 UK Punk Thatcherism, with detours into American 1968 counterculture, followed by '70–'80s New York avant-garde hegemony, created a symbolic continuum that placed the youth, and the newly available economic capital, at the center of the cultural conversation. In the history of advertising, things that were once created to cater to the needs of adults were now marketed to the youth. Moreover, the youth were now marketed as an image to instill the need to "be young" to a mass of aging adults. Today, things haven't changed much, and still, **THE CURRENCY OF YOUTH IS TRADED TO INVESTORS AND SHAREHOLDERS THROUGH EQUITY STAKES—MEANING: IF YOU BUY INTO IT, YOU'RE PART OF IT.**

This essay, at this point, is somehow expected to take a turn towards an exegesis of cultural and artistic expressions that have mapped and visualized the generational mythology of the youth. The essay, logically, would weave together a selected biography and context notes to several artworks, photographs, campaigns, exhibitions, and miscellaneous artifacts that, once agglomerated, reinforced the myth of the youth even further.**YES, MOTHER.**

A French artist. Disable AdBlock. Pyramid installation with beers that attendees can drink, hence no more pyramid at the end of the show. Click here to allow cookies. KW Institute of Contemporary Art, Berlin, 2011. Artforum.com—I accept. Cyprien Gaillard. You may also like: Dash Snow, *I Love You, Stupid*, 2013, 435 pages. Accept. Add to cart. Item sold out. Preface by Glenn O'Brien. Add to wishlist. Black and white polaroids of cool hip people doing wrong shit. A Turner Prize Winner. 1999. *BOOM!* Found-footage video. Fifteen minutes. Mark. Fucking. Leckey. *YEAH!* Literally sick kids dancing to sick tunes in a sick video. Acquired by Tate Modern and the Guggenheim, among others. A show-stopper. Who coined the YBA acronym? It stands for Young British Artists. A whole essay which is not this one. YOUNG! Damien Hirst, Tracey Emin, Goldsmiths, Royal College of Art, stuff like that... You just google it... Very young. Very British. Very artists. **MYTHOLOGIES LIKE I'M ROLAND BARTHES.** *BOOM!* Then what? Prince, that Richard fucking Prince. Everything. You choose. Same city, same crowd: the legendary Philip-Lorca diCorcia: goat. *ON GOD!* Germany, Europe, Anne Imhof and the gang, Wolfgang Tillmans before her, Michel Majerus before them both, and many more before many others. *SWAG ART!* Virgil Abloh in the same sentence as Raf Simons—an atrocity, according to the Belgian designer—but I fucking love it! Youth, and more youth. Everything is young, at some point, until it becomes old.

This is a Netflix trailer for an upcoming show. A pilot. A teaser. A 30-second snapshot of art history. Press here to watch. Pay us and we'll do it. TikTok snippets are cut from this. You think it's enough. It's fine. The theme is: Coming of Age. **BUT HOW CAN YOU COME OF AGE WHEN PEOPLE ARE COMING AFTER YOU AND YOUR GENERATIONAL VALUES?** How can you contribute to your generational poetics, still knowing that marketing executives, museum curators, magazine editors, heads of brands, and anything in between are buying into it without actually getting it? You wake up, get coffee or whatever you people take, and your "generational mythology" is turned into a series of Reels and TikToks, and, if you're lucky, an HBO mini-series. It's "Selling Sunset" but it's "Selling Something." It's "White Lotus" but it's "White Lot." It's "Euphoria" but it's "E for ya." It's "Emily in Paris" but it's "Emily on Heroin." It's "Sex and the City," but it's "Text in the City." Rewrite the narrative that's written for you—and for your generation. This is what a "coming of age" looks like. Something that the artists outlined above have explored, but that you have to discover without me explaining it. Otherwise, it's pointless. To the youth reading: I know you exist. I know you know. And mind that "youth" means nothing. But still, you don't want to be trapped in it. **YOU DON'T WANT TO BE YOUNG FOREVER FOR THE SAKE OF IT.** In the 5th century BC, a historian named Herodotus made a huge mistake: pretending that he had witnessed a mythical spring that supposedly restored the youth of anyone who drinks or bathes in its waters. Herodotus, everybody knows, was an imaginative man, and an impostor too; he thought that sources could be invented, and facts exaggerated—take, for example, when he reported that a fountain could turn you into your younger self. That's, for real, not true. Herodotus, like everyone, was "youth mythologizing"—selling those values to generational predecessors. We know how it goes.

The pronoun "you" and the word "youth" share the same root, I just realized. It must mean something. It's just like the "youth" extends the essence of the "you," at least linguistically. And semantically, that makes sense too. In reality, these two words share no common ground, but here in this context, they do. Let's rewind to the beginning: we call a generation "all the people of about the same age within a society or within a particular family." And this means a set of humans living around the same period of time.

To the youth reading: I hope you exist. I hope you know. And mind that "youth" is a trap. Don't buy into it. Generational mythology: to recap, it's when things shared and validated within a very very very very large group of people of the same age (aka a generation) are then transmitted and formalized for the entire world to consume. And the world is not just consuming it, it's feasting on it. Deal with it. This is your thing now. It's time for me to graduate, and for you to be the freshmen.

Late Greatest | Cusp | Early Silent | Core Silent

1924 1925 1926 — 1923 — 1924 1925 1926 — 1927 — 1928 1929 1930 — 1931 — 1932 1933 1934 1935 1936 — 1937

Late Silent | Cusp | Early Boomer | Core Boomer

1937 — 1938 1939 1940 — 1941 — 1942 1943 1944 — 1945 — 1946 1947 1948 — 1949 — 1950 1951 1952 1953 1954 — 1955

Late Boomer | Jones | Early X | Core X

1955 — 1956 1957 1958 — 1959 — 1960 1961 1962 — 1963 — 1964 1965 1966 — 1967 — 1968 1969 1970 1971 1972 — 1973

Late X | Xennial | Early Millennial | Core Millennial

1973 — 1974 1975 1976 — 1977 — 1978 1979 1980 — 1981 — 1982 1983 1984 — 1985 — 1986 1987 1988 1989 1990 — 1991

Late Millennial | Zillennial | Early Z | Core Z

1991 — 1992 1993 1994 — 1995 — 1996 1997 1998 — 1999 — 2000 2001 2002 — 2003 — 2004 2005 2006 2007 2008 — 2009

Late Z | Zalpha | Early Alpha | Core Alpha

2009 — 2010 2011 2012 — 2013 — 2014 2015 2016 — 2017 — 2018 2019 2020 — 2021 — 2022 2023 2024 2025 2026 — 2027

Late Alpha | Cusp | Early Beta

2027 — 2028 2029 2030 — 2031 — 2032 2033 2034 — 2035 — 2036 2037 2038

TULIPMANIA

What is it that keeps us all at work? Fame, sure. Glory, possibly. Gratification, very likely. Ego boost, why not. Money. During the era spanning from 1588 (the birth of the Dutch Republic) to 1672 (the "disaster year" in which France invaded and nearly overran the Dutch Republic), the Netherlands acquired significant economic power, becoming the fulcrum of trade, science, and art in Europe and beyond. One of the major Atlantic slave-trading nations, with a share of an average of around five percent, at least 500,000 people. During this period, dubbed the "Dutch Golden Age," economic liberty set the blueprint for modern neoliberalism emphasizing free markets, free trade, and private property under free enterprise. Hot take: capitalism and its political structure were devised, perfected, and lastly put in place during that period.

Together with the birth of modern capitalism, the world needed more sophisticated commodities to trade, goods that could be exchanged with arbitrarily inflated prices, resulting in consistent markups in sales:

capitalism 101. What else could have provided this opportunity, if not works of art, specifically, paintings? According to British writer Jonathan Israel, it has been roughly estimated that over 1.3 million Dutch pictures were painted in the 20 years after 1640 alone, but this was not enough for artists to make decent numbers. Artists like Vermeer, Frans Hals, and Rembrandt were poor in life and died poorer. In the 17th-century art market, the supply of paintings exceeded the demand—dealers learned only in future years that scarcity inflates the demand for luxury goods.

Something else was perfected and put into place during that time: tulips. The first bulbs of tulips were introduced from the Ottoman Empire to Europe around 1554 and became increasingly popular in the Netherlands during the 16th and 17th centuries. Due to their novelty features, such as bright colors and exotic provenance, **TULIPS WERE SOUGHT BY THE DUTCH ARISTOCRACY AND BOURGEOISIE ALMOST AS A COLLECTIBLE ITEM.**

The species soon came to symbolize luxury and wealth, coincidentally driven by Holland's rising economy and wealthy families at the helm of commerce, culture, and society. Many varieties of these spring-blooming perennial herbaceous bulbiferous geophytes came into the market, each with a different colorway, name, and quality. With the market flooded by tulip bulbs, the demand kept growing. **SHIT GOT SPECULATIVE.** Tulip traders in Europe paid the higher and higher price of bulbs, with value growing steadily. The steadily rising prices tempted many ordinary middle-class and poor families to speculate in the tulip market. Homes, estates, and industries were mortgaged so that bulbs could be bought for resale at higher prices.

Tulip mania reached its peak during the winter of 1636–37, when contracts were changing hands five times. It is said that a Viceroy Tulip was worth upwards of five times the cost of an average house at the time. No deliveries were ever made to fulfill any of these contracts, because in February 1637, tulip bulb contract prices collapsed abruptly, and the trade of tulips ground to a halt. This dramatic curve caused the market to collapse, with the exchanged goods surpassing their intrinsic value, hence instigating a market bubble.

Historians still debate whether "tulipmania" can actually be considered a market bubble; it definitely is a phenomenon of collective craze for luxury products. Tulips had no practical function or implication per se (no, you can't make heroin out of tulips. Those are poppies!), if not providing the tangible image of the spending power of the wealthiest class of the richest country in 17th-century Europe. In the economical framing of the phenomenon, the bubble might have been burst by irrationally inflated prices that led speculation to become a market crash, but on the other side of the coin, we see how social trends are much more volatile than market prices. If tulips approximated to currency for some, they became a symbol of class status for others, but not forever.

The social counterpart of the tulip bubble resides in the crucial, yet simple observation that Dutch **RICH HOUSEWIVES GOT BORED BY EXOTIC BULBS**, multicolored floral arrangements, and paintings depicting both subjects, and moved on to something else. Cultural indicators change as culture evolves together with its symbols. Identification via cultural objects is not a monolithic process set in stone, but rather an ephemeral mechanism whose symbolic commodities have a fixed expiration date, and even more so in the luxury market, where products that convey status follow a vertiginous exhaustion cycle until they're emptied of their cultural capital and are rendered as completely meaningless until a new social group collectively decides to attribute them further cultural relevance. This is not far from the case of, let's say, a prototype pair of all-black Nike Air Yeezys worn by Kanye

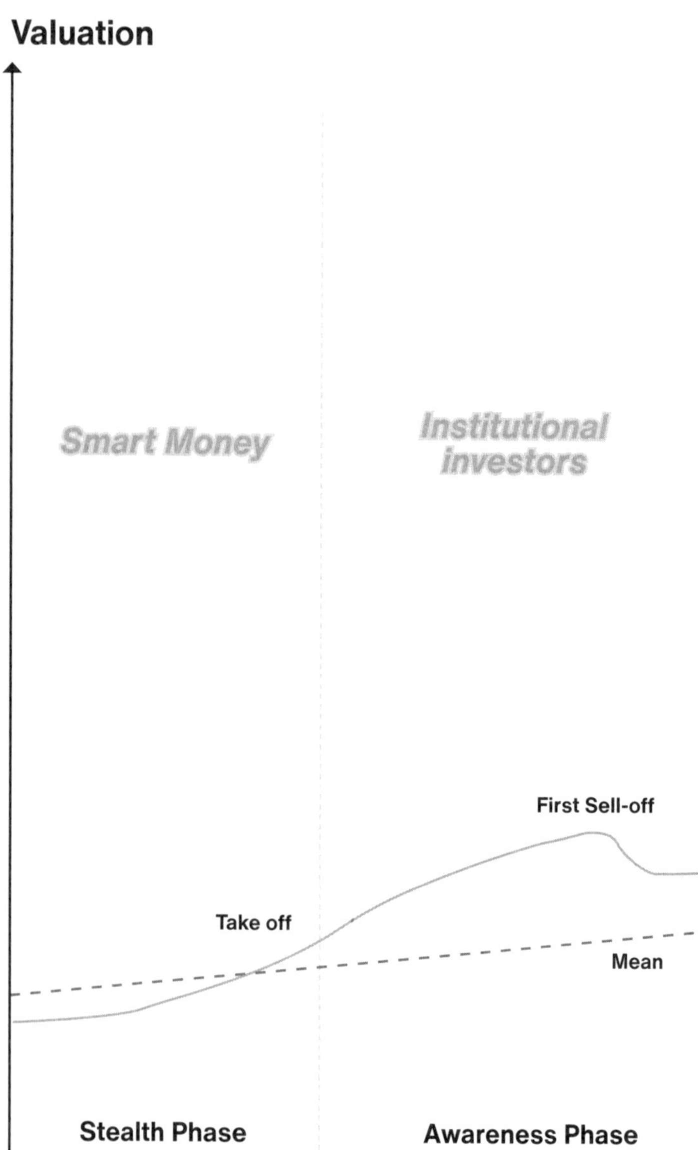

Valuation
Smart Money
Institutional investors
First Sell-off
Take off
Mean
Stealth Phase
Awareness Phase

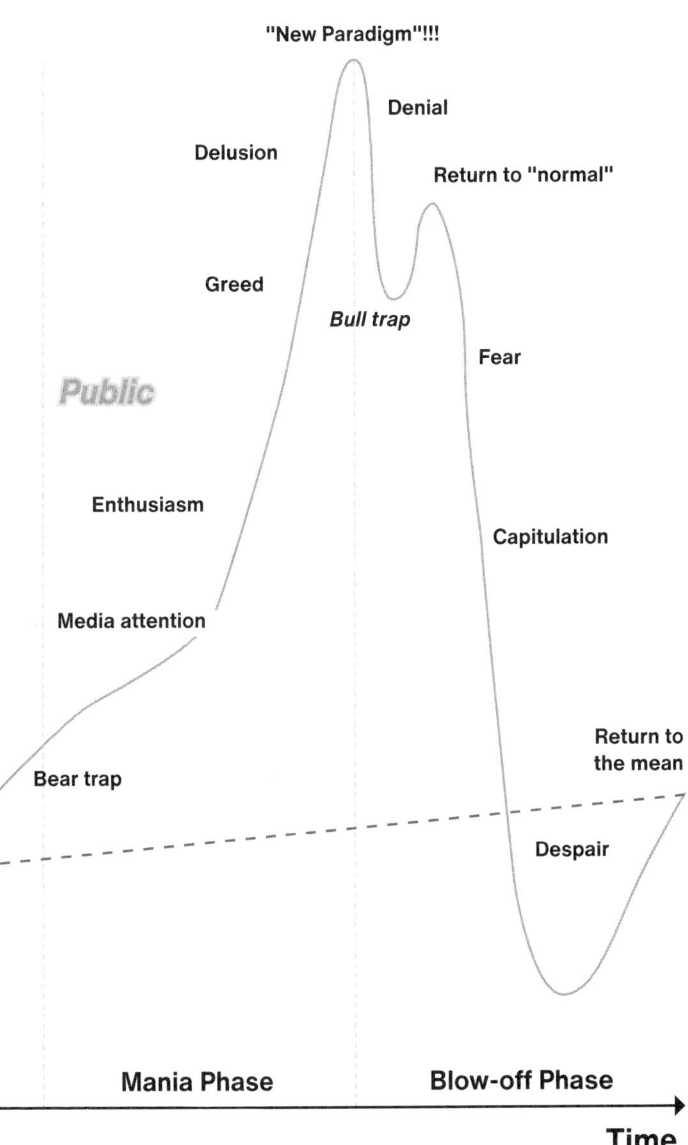

"New Paradigm"!!!
Denial
Delusion
Return to "normal"
Greed
Bull trap
Fear
Public
Enthusiasm
Capitulation
Media attention
Return to
the mean
Bear trap
Despair
Mania Phase
Blow-off Phase
Time

West at the 2008 Grammy Awards sold for $1,800,000 by Sotheby's, or a collection of any brand in 2030 when indiesleaze or gorpcore will be prehistoric concepts.

In a superlative scene painted by Jan Brueghel the Younger in 1640, we see monkeys performing tasks associated with the trade of tulip bulbs. The painting, titled *Satire of Tulipomania*, adheres to the stylistic conventions of the trope of the singerie, in which monkeys were used as allegorical characters to convey moral judgment and dubious traits of human behavior. The "monkey scene" genre developed as a metaphorical tool to mock certain attitudes, facts, and events of the present or recent past in the style of cultural commentary. The painting shows primates caught exchanging bulbs, cataloging their prices, feasting under a colonnaded lodge, counting money on a red-clothed table, weighing bulbs, and even pissing on them. Silly little monkeys with silly little tasks—except, those were, fundamentally, humans.

Jan Brueghel the Younger was a nepo baby. Actually, the ultimate nepo baby—son of Jan Brueghel the Elder, grandson of the mega-master Pieter Bruegel the Elder. This didn't prevent "Lil Brueghel" from going beyond the rural-landscape formalism his paintings often transuded to paint a playfully enigmatic scene that would speak to future generations forever. *Satire of Tulipomania* might be a highly tropey allegory commenting on a crazy market bubble, but it is, ultimately, the depiction of the death of a trend. Its funeral. Its aftermath. The mourning of the followers of a now-defunct trend. A derisive monument to groupthink and its implication in today's luxurified social ecosystem. An oil-on-canvas mockery of trends, their followers, and their initiators. **A BIG, MUSEUM-CONSERVED, CENTURY-LASTING "FUCK YOU" TO YOUR SILLY, CLICK-BAITED VIBE SHIFT.**

An economic bubble, to classify as such, must fulfill the following characteristics, or stages: unusual changes in single measures (i.e., prices) relative to their historical levels;

elevated usage of debt to purchase assets; higher risk lending and borrowing behavior; making decisions based on expected future price increases rather than the ability of the borrower to repay; a high presence of marketing or media coverage related to the asset. Feels familiar? Three hundred eighty-six years away from the infamous tulip bubble and its subsequent crash, yet we're still at the mercy of unusual shifts in prices relative to historical levels, elevated usage of debt

(KLARNA

IS

DEBT, BUDDY!),

making decisions based on future prices (archival baby!), and, of course, the high presence of marketing and media coverage that never went away. Call me Lil Brueghel!

In KAWS's 2005 painting *THE KAWS ALBUM*, we witness the double detournement of one of the most iconic images of recent popular culture. Characters of the group shot gracing the cover of The Beatles's eighth studio album *Sgt. Pepper's Lonely Hearts Club Band* are not only replaced by

Simpsons figures, but those characters are in turn KAWSified to create a weird hybrid that the artist has dubbed "Kimpsons." Not only are we witnessing a three-layered pop-cultural inception nightmare, but we're at the same time discussing a painting sold at Sotheby's for $14.7 million. The composition of the painting, and its subjects, relate to an extremely mundane dimension, where its characters are performing a group pose conveying simple and direct personification: they simply perform themselves, in a group.

Through the Beatles–Simpsons–Kimpsons pipeline, the image acquires an allegorical quality by which it could be read as a metaphor for pop culture in its entirety—quite a simple dynamic, yet a powerful one. Allegorically speaking, those are monkeys posing metaphorically as humans—a semiotic jump, if you like, very much facilitated by KAWS's signature figurines and their formal resemblance to exaggeratedly unproportioned primates. The work in question, if not formally, but at least conceptually, participates in and advances the historicized trope of the singerie (or "monkey scene") in which human life provides the topic for cultural commentary. And, just as the picture Jan Brueghel the Younger painted in 1640, this painting acts as the key element in the commentary of an economic bubble that's happening in society at the same time. *THE KAWS ALBUM*, and its record-breaking sale from its previous owner Nigo—ironically enough, the founder of the brand A Bathing Ape—is the ultimate funeral of a trend. And its KAWS–Simpsons–Beatles weird hybrid allegorical monkeys are there to play the same function as Bruegel's: making fun of us..

Making fun of tulips was so much easier for Brueghel than for KAWS—still unsure if this is the artist's intent, or just mine. Tulips, in the Dutch Golden Age, can be regarded as placeholder symbols for vanity and wealth, self-contained objects that served only the purpose of identifying their owners into the same cultural class. Today is way harder than that. Tulipmania can be translated into today under the form of many different specific niche manias: algo-mania, sneaker-mania, self-mania, and so on, all piling up to define millennial schizophrenia and community-induced paranoia. Our tulips are not just tulips, but the entire spectrum of knowledgeable botany; we in the first place do not know what we specifically crave, but we do. Once one placeholder- **TULIP-CULTURAL-OBJECT** is gone, we wait for another one to come up, to blossom from a motherfucking bulb.

EXQUISITE BOURGEOISIE

"That you who are reading this are reading it is almost proof in itself: proof that you belong." German theorist Hans Magnus Enzensberger wrote this passage in his 1976 Marxist-adjacent essay "On the Inevitability of the Middle Classes." For Enzensberger, the bourgeoisie could only be defined in terms of what it is not, as the class that is neither nor.

To claim a univocal definition of the bourgeoisie is, indeed, a paradox, as the term has been twisted and mystified throughout history—first, gaining political status through the French revolution, then translating into the subtle form of lifestyle throughout the 20th century. Inevitably, with the developments of late capitalism and the rise of the immaterial economy, which complicated the direct relation between product and capital, the bourgeoisie itself became a condition, rather than a class.

"Class," "classic," "classy": the semantics around the bourgeoise ideal come as no surprise with connotations of elegance, luxury, grandiosity, and, again, **CLASS (AS IN CHIC)** reinforcing the historicized belief of the upper-middle class as the only arbiter of taste, the gatekeeper of dignity, the ultimate ruling social group—something that critical theory has defined as a cultural hegemony.

The version of the bourgeoisie I have come to understand and be aware of is extremely localized within a 3+ kilometer radius with a fixed perimeter, both architectural and social. This version has nothing to do with money or assets, but with habit and comfort: an idea rather than a fact, a curse, and not a privilege, and, to use the most petit-bourgeois expression ever, something that's *in the details.*

Slow, easy, and extremely mundane, the everyday becomes a viable form of entertainment for a dazed jet-set of unrevolutionary characters, whose lives evolve in a predictable loophole of uneventful dichotomies—**THEY SPIN IN CIRCLES, GRAVITATE AT MODEST SPEED AROUND AN INSIGNIFICANT YET DIGESTIBLE ORBIT OF HABITS.**

Milan: a city that's more understandable in terms of geometry than geography. The city's circles—Roman fortifications evolved into feudal walls—expand from the central nucleus through a series of concentric rings that progressively divide the city center from its periphery. By design, Milan is a spiraling city, a blueprint for gated urbanism.

Through repetition, the historically preserved layout of the city has allowed the creation of a certain kind of spirit that infiltrates every aspect of the Milanese routine today. The Milan ethos is a bourgeois ethos, a set of parameters and indicators of a peculiar sensibility that is shared among different generations and walks of life.

As citizens of the same city, we are all guilty of the non-progressiveness we have caused. As members of the same generation, we are all guilty of the revolution we have never caused. Things don't change, have never changed, and still, the bourgeois pattern of behavior drives us on autopilot.

In her 1990 essay "About Piero & Me," the late architect Nanda Vigo elaborated a sentimental account of her relationship with her partner, the artist Piero Manzoni, and his tragic death in 1963 at the age of 29. That piece, which reads like an intimate diary entry, is as much a love letter to the late artist as it is to the city of Milan and its social dynamics. Manzoni died of a heart attack in his studio, allegedly having drunk himself to death after a night spent drifting around Milan's Brera district with a posse of fellow companions, artists, and intellectuals. Manzoni and Vigo's routine unfolded within a set of fixed coordinates that rarely extended outside of Brera, and involved a great deal of bar-hopping, late-night dinners, and fierce dissatisfaction with pretty much everything.

For a long time, I've been thinking of this essay as the ultimate documentation of a bourgeois tragedy that unraveled with sorrow, yet grace, in an ironic twist of events—the man who was supposed to change everything, and subvert the intrinsic hierarchy in contemporary culture, lies dead in his studio, killed by the pathetic, well-educated, unglamorous, intellectually-charged, bourgeois script he adapted his life to. Not even Manzoni himself managed to start that revolution.

Milan hasn't changed much since then, and my peers and I have accepted the challenge of pretending to be rich. We are the Beat generation without a beat; we are the Situationists without situations, the Futurists with no future. We are a parody of industrialism and church-versus-state pedigree;

WE ARE LIVING
POSTCODES
AND NOTHING ELSE.

Milan is our muse—detached, frigid, unreadable—and so is its code: an instruction manual that's not included in the box, a gossip column from a cheap Italian tabloid, a trope made of expensive furniture and ugly buildings. The truth is: no one gives a fuck about Milan. And to be honest, neither do I.

In music criticism, ambient is a genre that emphasizes tone and atmosphere over traditional musical structure or rhythm—a form of instrumental music that may lack composition, beat, or structured melody. In architecture, Angelo Lunati defines *ambiente* (ambiance) as the "space that surrounds a person or a thing," with connotations of circularity due to the Greek prefix "amphi-"—as in amphitheater—which implicates a path that's "all around." In his book *Ideas of Ambiente: History and Bourgeois Ethics in the Construction of Modern Milan*, Lunati aims at defining Milan's *ambiente* as the overarching quality in the development of the bourgeoisie metropolis.

Milan is an ambient city whose concentric skeleton reinforced a class division that is mostly aesthetic rather than political, where the lack of ideology in architecture had contributed to the formation of the city's distinctive character—an idea so deeply rooted within Milan's social fabric that not even the 1970s avant-garde managed to destroy it. I wonder if BBPR, Gae Aulenti, Aldo Rossi, or the *Casabella* crew would understand how their disruptive work exists today as the new bourgeoisie memento: poor rich kids and their posh thrift stores.

The Holy Trinity of the Bourgeoisie

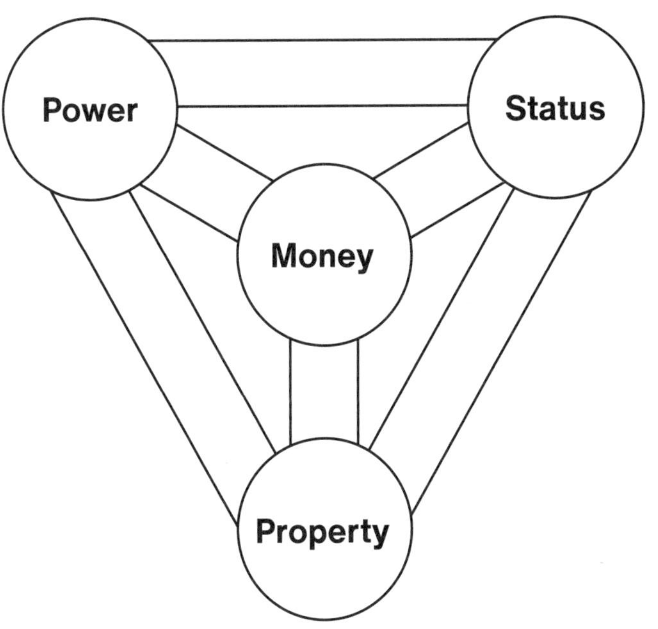

And yet, I have spent a great deal of time at my friends' houses this year and, as in a temporal loop, I keep sitting on an always different, yet same, version of an Aulenti or Castiglioni armchair. This is clearly the aesthetic token we have been left with: the gold standard of Milanese life.

Last year, I became obsessed with a 1908 self-portrait by Umberto Boccioni, one of the very few the artist painted. In the work, the artist is portrayed on his balcony overlooking the Milanese countryside, where he'd moved to escape urban stress. One year later, in 1909, Filippo Tommaso Marinetti published his "Futurist Manifesto" and mailed it around Europe with a return address no further than one kilometer from Boccioni's balcony. From Boccioni's balcony, you can also see the building where I lived for three years.

The posh countryside had been counter-gentrified since Boccioni's day, meaning that the rich have been kicked out of the neighborhood by the poor, who weren't seeking refuge from urban stress as the painter did. That's not a process that you get to see often in New York or London. We, the poor turned aesthetically bourgeois, keep this neighborhood for ourselves, but we still have to negotiate the upper-class aesthetics embedded in the area. Again, Lunati's definition of *ambiente* as a complex network that transcends architecture to incorporate lifestyle, as an all-encompassing experiential dimension, provides context to the cyclical reinvention of bourgeois spaces.

MILAN:
WONDERFUL PALACE,
MEDIOCRE LOVER.

This year, I moved 500 meters away from Boccioni's balcony. From mine, now, I can see the apartment of the photographer who shot this story, as well as the headquarters of the PR firm that facilitated it. In this insignificant portion of the universe, no manifesto has ever been written and I doubt it will be anytime soon because we don't need one.

Manifestos—organized or informal declarations of intentions for purposes of divulgation and historicization—have heavily informed the research of critical design studio Experimental Jetset around radical art movements. In their recently published book *Superstructures*, the collective distills the revolutionary embodiment of historical avant-gardes within the Modernist city. Four models emerge from their analysis: the Constructivist city, the Situationist city, the Provotarian city, and the Post-Punk city. Although each of these models has specific characteristics derived from each of the movements, they all provide a reading of the cityscape as an extension of language. A Roland Barthes quote introduces the preface: "The city is a discourse, and this discourse is actually a language: the city speaks to its inhabitants, as we speak to our city..."

The language we speak here is the codified language of the bourgeoisie, as the ultimate conceptual detournement of status. We don't speak it to our city but to ourselves. And if the discourse is actually a language, as per Barthes, our conversation with the city is overheard across coffee tables, politely intellectualized around late-'70s sofa setups, repeated over and over incessantly through ideas and actions, embedded within a mode of behavior. Milan and its circles, ideas and actions, embedded within a mode of behavior. Milan and its circles.

49

LIL WHITE BAG (SKIT)

SNIFF! SNAFF! GRUNT! POW!   This is no comic strip and no one has superpowers (yet). I'm not listening. You're not listening. We're an ensemble of mouths and sounds orchestrated to produce a chaotically engineered cacophony. We're composing in counterpoint—or, the relationship between two or more musical lines that are harmonically interdependent, yet independent in rhythm and melodic contour. Like Bach, Wagner, Stravinsky, Cage, etc. We don't move in the same direction, we're univocal, obstinate voices arranged   **TO CREATE   DISSONANCE.** We're not good. Just like me with writing. But still, tonight, we have things to say. Apparently.

Left a "cool" job in my late twenties. Felt exploited, unhappy. Whose house is this? Weird that you mention it: Dan Graham was also an Aries and he was obsessed. RIP. I have no clue about astrology, I just know that when people ask me my sign, they give me that weird look of disapproval when I say "Aries," and then say something like "Ha!" He wrote:

"Aries, child of the zodiac, is perpetually over-compensating for its fragile sense of self with an extremely large ego." Graham also wanted to be a writer more than anything. He also said that Warhol, too, wanted to be a writer. He also did a performance titled *Don't Trust Anyone Over Thirty*. I know, three-zero, right?

I feel so old. In fact, I feel ancient. I feel historical, that's a good way to put it. Years pass, and still, we keep reiterating a simulation of Gertrude Stein's salon, on crack. **TRAP SALONS?** Someone should write about it. "The Trap House as a Salon," something that I would publish if I didn't have to write it myself. But it's true, the same models of cultural production—although way more instinctive and definitely not self-intellectu-alized—are reiterated and progress in time through aggregation and social organization. Lock a group of people up in a room and they will do stuff. Stuff is culture.

This night. An impressionist travelogue. Henry Miller's *The Colossus of Maroussi*. An unreliable narrator. Confused syntax residu-al of a modernist novel. An amorphous blob;

The Listening Cycle

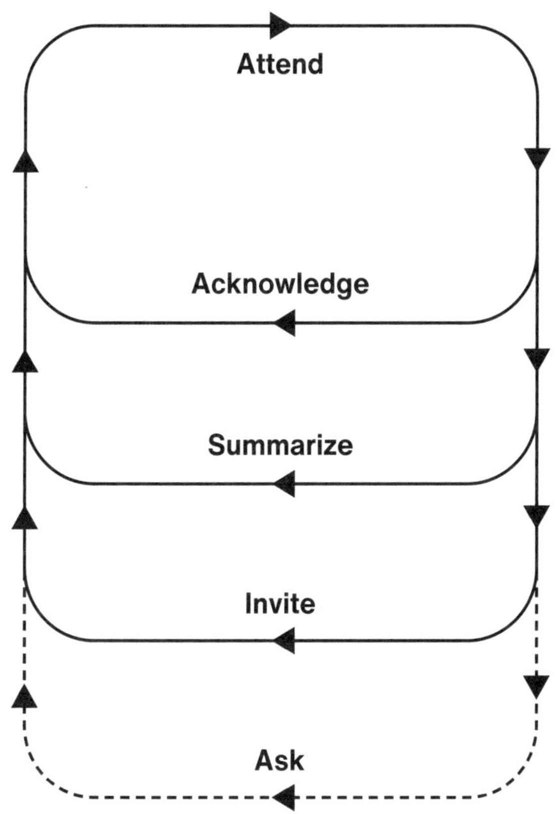

the plot sunk in the background; subjectivity; our night goes by and we talk, talk, talk, talk. **SNIFF! SNAFF! GRUNT! POW!** This is no Playboi Carti but the soundtrack of a deranged yet very controlled house party. Bags bags bags but we're not talking Telfars. Pathetic. Oh yeah, I used to live there, it's nice! Eight years, yeah, it's a long time for a shitty city like this. I'm good, I'm good, thanks. How are you and oh-my-god-I-totally-forgot-her-name doing? Oh, I know this track. Oh, I have this book. Oh, I've seen you walking by. Oh, I follow you. Oh, we should definitely hang out more. Oh, we should totally hang out more. Oh, I'll text you tomorrow. Oh, we'll have a drink tomorrow. Oh, let's meet at 7 pm tomorrow.

Tomorrow. Tomorrow. Tomorrow. To more morrows. Too morrows.

Imagine going home late in the night, feeling wasted, lying in bed, eyes closed, brain dead, thinking: "I've had too many tomorrows!" Yeah, tomorrow I'll feel great. Tomorrow I'm gonna meet oh-my-god-I-totally-forgot-her-and-his-names and we'll have a great time! Tomorrow I'm gonna send emails. Tomorrow, I'm gonna do it tomorrow. But it's still "today"—although 5 am—and things don't look trap-house, but more trapped-in-the-house. House arrest. Narcotic lockdown. A gym for mouths, voices, and saliva: instead of weights we lift words with the same intensity. A power-wired choir. We do squats over a glass side table prepped with paraphernalia. We do cardio. We sweat through Jil Sander white tees. We integrate several integrators. We gain mass and we lose fat. We box but through dialogue: interlocutors MMA'd only by the noblest move of talking without listening at all; partners Ju-Jitsu'd by a non-stop burst of questions; guests Muay-Thai'd by fun facts, irrelevant information, and theories. And then, of course, my turn to take in all the shots.

IT'S ALL HEAVENLY RECIPROCAL: THE ART OF CONVERSATIONAL GYMNASTICS.

SNIFF! SNAFF! GRUNT! POW! This is no Roy Lichtenstein and this shit is not sold at Sotheby's. Oh yeah, sure, they can come! Hey, it's the third floor, elevator on the left. Hiiii, nice to see you! Thank you, thank you, yeah, it's great, we love it here, we moved in two years ago! This one? We got it for reeeal cheap, it was a steal, we just changed the lightbulb and it was practically new. Yeah, I've had a couple of those too. Yes! It's a Warhol print editioned by Castelli, an auction find! Thank you! Wade Guyton, a poster he made for a show in Paris. Sick, yes! You know I've never even typed a word on that desk? I've looked for it for years, but, I must say, it's as beautiful as it is useless. A guy who worked at Olivetti brought it with a van. Of course, no problem, love a little house tour! Ohhhhhh, you shouldn't have! Yeah, of course, it's chill! On the glass side table, make yourself at home.

Eyes are triggered. Pupils awaken. What time is it? Foreheads shine. *Did we call again?* Mouths are dry. Teeth grind. Jaws max out. *Hey do you have any cash?* Chests stiffen. Legs cross. *A small one!* Backs lay. Arms vibrate.

Here, use this! Hands gesticulate. *Love the wine!* Ears filter. Feet stand. *Hey, where is the music playing from?* Noses, busy. Tongues swallow. *What's your passcode?* Livers hustle. *Yeah, no, so I was telling you ...* Bladders store. *Omg, I'm so sorry, did I break it?* Lungs hit. *Do you have a cigarette?* Hearts pump.

We have a problem. Houston. Not Texas. "Paris, Texas" is in the bio of someone I'm talking to right now. "Milano, Texas" is on the skin of someone else I'm talking to right now. "Houston, Texas" is in the lyrics of some track someone I'm talking to right now has Bluetooth'd onto the speakers right now. Right now. Everything, right now. Right. Now. It's either right now or never. It's either right now or tomorrow. Is it right? It's just right now.

Right now, I could I should I would I might I will. It's not that everything is possible, but that everything is right now. Until it lasts, until cabs are called, until all the glass side tables are clean, until belongings previously scattered around are re-belonged, until cigarettes are fully ash-trayed, until plates

recommence to serve their designated function, until banknotes are un-rolled. Until
right now it's not right anymore.

SELECTED AMBIENT WORKS

Is your child texting about "ambient?" brb = background reverb broadcast; stfu = soundscapes to feel universal; lol = loungewear or leave; lmao = let's meditate and overshare; idc = immersive deprivation cure; wtf = wellness transcendence friday; smh = soft millennial homeware. Need more signs? Pale colors, homewear, gradient tones, shareable flat infographics, reassuring typography, algorithm-assembled infinite playlists, lack of narrative, immersive installations, neon lights, pseudomeditative hot yoga sessions, beige sweatpants, gallery rooms filled with field recordings, Web3-ish colorful blobs; soundscapes of sorts, pseudo-minimalism, Donda-architecture… the list is literally endless. Your child, along with everybody else, is definitely texting about ambient—and they might not be aware yet.

If Thoreau knew that in writing *Walden* in 1854 he might incidentally be considered the inventor and perpetrator of "ambient," we wouldn't live in a world where listening to the sounds of nature is a thing. The phrase "listening to the sounds of nature," here, works as a metaphor for a renewed, precise aesthetic attunement widely diffused among the global millennial demographics. In the same semantic framework—that of cheap synesthesia—the act of listening to nature might as well stand for additional placeholder clichès like "tasting the world," "living in colors," "visualizing a smell." **AMBIENT WORKS WITHIN THE MECHANICS OF SYNESTHESIA, AS IT'S A QUALITY THAT CAN BE APPLIED ACROSS THE SENSORY OR COGNITIVE SPECTRUM— THE VISUAL, THE SONIC, THE BEHAVIORAL, THE EXPERIENTIAL, THE ENVIRONMENTAL.**

Ambient is "as ignorable as it is interesting," as the musician Brian Eno wrote when he coined the term "ambient music" in the liner notes to his 1978 album *Ambient 1: Music for Airports,* "intended to induce calm and a space to think." More than a music genre, ambient is a quality, a specific trope applicable to the entire spectrum of cultural production, and beyond. From music, literature, cinema, art, and fashion, to urbanism, product design, and architecture, the term "ambient" relates to the immediate surroundings of something. French composer Erik Satie coined the term "furniture music" (musique d'ameublement) in 1917, while John Cage repurposed this concept in his 1952 work *4'33"*. Beyond music, the same "ambient" characteristics can be found in environmental art, large-scale installations, found footage collages, field-recording soundscapes, ecological practices and studies, James Turrell-inspired hip hop videos, binge able Netflix shows, infinite Spotify playlists, the rising popularity of dissociative substances, and the infinite scroll of social media.

The shift from ambient music to ambient everything is real. Previously dismissed as an atmospheric, textural soundtrack playing in the background of your daily life, ambient re-emerges as the central aesthetics of the early '20s, perhaps as an instinctive reaction to the global inherent chaos. Ambient stops signaling the surrounding environment—as per its traditional coinage—to become interiorized and self-reflective: a form of self-centered empathy, an embodied sim-ulation of our better self. Everything could fall under the characterization of ambient, the term being wide and open enough to fit the complexity of the now.

WE'RE LIVING AMBIENT-MODE.

In her essay "Sculpture in the Expanded Field," published in *October* Vol. 8 (Spring, 1979), American art critic Rosalind Krauss distills the heterogeneity of the universally accepted definition of "sculpture" to subvert the inherent logic of the medium, until then applied within the limits of representation in the sculptural form. With Krauss—and the cluster of artists she references in the essay, such as Richard Serra, Robert Morris, Mary Miss, Robert Smithson, among others—the sculptural logic is problematized to the point that the medium ceases to be situated in a relation of direct opposition—sculpture is neither landscape nor architecture—to become freed from its own physical–objec-tual constraints.

Not only does Krauss's essay provide context to the expansion of sculpture—and

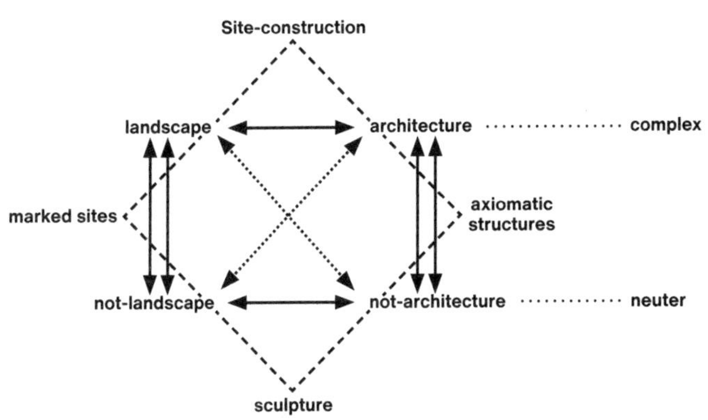

Site-construction
landscape
architecture
complex
marked sites
axiomatic
structures
not-landscape
not-architecture
neuter
sculpture

postmodern aesthetics—outside of the space-time axiom, but it also develops a new language, a new terminology to address this shift. Semantically, the essay makes use of words that seem to adhere to the sphere of the fluid, the flexible, the open. "Expanded," "manipulation," "elasticity," "field," "suspended" are all words implying the possibility of the formal and theoretical expansion of that precise artistic medium. This vocabulary comes in handy here to raise questions that prompt a similar reflection on expansion in the auratic field of experience.

After Krauss, a lot of things happened in the expanded field, which, to clarify, is not a physical space and/or container, but a diagrammatic matrix created by mathematician Christian Felix Klein in 1884 to denote a group with four elements, in which each element is self-inverse. If the Klein four-group in Krauss's work served as an explainer for the expansion of sculpture beyond the is-it-landscape-or-architecture complex, a similar conceptual approach was put into action by Nicolas Bourriaud in his 1998 book

Relational Aesthetics. Here, the French critic studies the recurring patterns within a specific group of artists operating at the nexus of sculpture, installation, and interactivity. The participatory, expansive nature of many of the works Borriaud took into account—by Rikrit Tiravanija, Carsten Höller, Liam Gillick, and Philippe Parreno, among others—pushed the critic to postulate a new mode in a set of artistic practices that "take as their theoretical and practical point of departure the whole of human relations," expanding outside the traditional, pre-fixed limits of the space–object lineage, while still retaining a physicality—or materiality.

Unlike Conceptual Art, for example, Relational Art had nothing to do with immateriality. If anything, it had to do with artworks spreading out of their material form (while still having one). But this is not to say that form is here intended as pure rigidity: in relational practices, form is in the exchange; form is residual of the exchange. In the relational mode, artists like Philippe Parreno, Dominique Gonzalez-Foerster, and Pierre

Huyghe, expanded their works not only to the point of creating environments, but conditions. The work is site-specific in its purest terms: if it's here, it's the work; if you're here, it's the work. But... here, where? In order for the work to exist, or do its job, you'll have to immerse. Here, in, and within the experience.

It's here that the expansive *immersivity* interjects in the ambient mythmaking pipeline. It's logical to say that works that shared the same theoretical milieux reflected this association also aesthetically, building a visual vocabulary that grouped even further the practices of this group of artists. Neon lights flooding the gallery space; light walls irradiating white cubes with flat, fluorescent tones; gradient palettes filtered through natural light; natural, earthly elements brought inside the museum; atmospheric agents; soft surfaces; soundscapes. The aesthetics are clear and reminiscent of the historicized legacy of Minimalism, but what it's new is that art functions as a container, a background, for human relations. This tendency is further emphasized by a new generation of artists operating across sound and installation like Sandra Mujinga, Klein, Lamin Fofana, Chino Amobi, and Precious Okoyomon, whose practices reflect a renewed interest in the spiritual, meditative, collective element.

Not unlike Eno's formulation of ambient music as background music, relational art paved the way for a new typology of artworks that acted as both the content and the context, shifting the perspective from making art to experiencing art. A similar view is expressed by musician and author David Toop in his seminal 1995 book *Ocean of Sound* (again, ambient synesthesia), in which he writes about how Brian Eno "applied the term 'ambient music' to his activities, switching the emphasis away from making music, focusing instead on the act of listening." The theoretical dismantling of the producer-consumer—or the artist-visitor—complex ushers us right into the age of the expanded experience.

Another product of the mid-'90s, the essay "Welcome to the Experience Economy," published in the *Harvard Business*

Review (July–August 1998), illustrates how commodities are fungible, goods tangible, services intangible, and experiences memorable. The essay predicts a vast majority of the recent developments in consumption—the retail experience, customer immersion, service commodities—setting the blueprint for a newly reconfigured economic system (immersive capitalism?).

What about today? If we accelerate Bourriaud's *Relational Aesthetics*, filtered through Krauss's expanded field, reverberated by the totalizing experience economy, and compressed by the algorithmic sovereignty of social media and digital products, we get "ambient."

Ambient as feed; ambient as medicine to millennial toxic paranoia; ambient as the entropic response to collective mood shifts; ambient as aesthetics; ambient as vibe; **AMBIENT AS MOOD—BUT VIA THE TUMBLR-ESQUE URGE TO WRITE WITH EXTRA SPACING IN BETWEEN LETTERS: M O O D.**

Like a field-recorded soundscape reverberating within a gallery space, or a soothing, washed-out blue neon light, we, ourselves, have become the background. Everything we do is in the background; we exist ambient-mode in the age of the expanded feed. We are served exhibitions that look like our feed, to consume our feed within. We are given immersive experiences that look like—excuse the naivety—the internet, to scroll the internet within. We are given TV shows that look like our Instagram profile, to scroll meanwhile. We are given "essential" clothes with the word "essential" written on top, hence being no longer essential. We are part of the surrounding, we are in the background, and such product-experiences incentivize us to do so. We have Emily in Paris but we are Paris. Everything fades off into feed.

According to a report issued on March 8, 2022 by Allied Market Research, the global antidepressant market size is forecast to reach $21 billion by 2030, seeing selective serotonin reuptake inhibitors as the leading segment. On the other hand, "doomscrolling" features as one of the highlighted trends in Google's "Year in Search 2021" report, while Peter Thiel-backed psychedelic start-up Atai Life Sciences gets authorized by the U.S. Food and Drug Administration to conduct a clinical trial on a nonpsychedelic form of ketamine for treatment-resistant depression. In March 2021, Otsuka Pharmaceutical announced a $20 million licensing agreement to develop and commercialize Perception's R-ketamine compound in Japan as a potential treatment for major depressive disorder and treatment-resistant depression. Peak dissociation intersects ambient as we transition from spa treatment to ketamine sauna-meets-emotional detox center, dressed in low-impact sweatsuits ranging from Cobalt Blue, Saffron Yellow, and Flamingo Pink to Celestial Blue, Orchid Purple, and Jade Green.

We're living in a Pantone of the Year-tinged simulation, the ultimate kingdom of mood. It's still unclear whether we are in an egg-shaped sensory isolation tank or in an egg-shaped, space-age toilet of a Michelin three-star restaurant in Mayfair, London. The truth is: everything is shaped like an egg now, if not formally, at least conceptually. Simple, rounded, oval, smooth, flawless, pale, innocent, organic, and yet, at the same time, at the epicenter of an old-as-time philosophical conundrum, as well as the primary commodity of a global market that, according to research firm IndexBox, is forecast to reach 138 million tons by 2030.

The year is 2022. Your whole Twitter talks about "a vibe shift"; a new Web3, DAO-ish start-up named something like "AuraTM" pops up on the market by the hour; incense burners sell out on luxury e-commerce retailers; the "Immersive Van Gogh" blockbuster traveling exhibition-franchise sells about 4.5 million tickets, translating into roughly $250 million in revenue; The artist formerly known as Kanye West performs his 10th studio album in an apocalyptic setting with halogen lights reflecting on the flooded floor, while an Olafur Eliasson-reminiscent semicircular screen and artificial mist create the illusion of a sun. I haven't thought so much about aura since 2015 when I was a presumptuous theory-and-butter criticism student approaching Walter Benjamin as I assume everyone did: bad & lazy. But today, really, everything is about aura.

AURA

IS THE ULTIMATE BRANDING
FOR OUR GENERATION

a spectrum of products, images, and practices that absorbs us without knowing we're fading off into background noise.

NEW! WRITING! NOW!

List of all the tasks I've ever performed, and the job roles I've ever impersonated (although having never been formally employed once in my life) throughout my career: art critic, music critic, fashion critic, culture critic, art writer, music writer, fashion writer, culture writer, copywriter, ghostwriter, curator, associate curator, assistant curator, curatorial assistant, gallery assistant, gallery intern, museum guide, editor in chief, associate editor, assistant editor, editorial assistant, library guy, bookshop weekend-shift guy, publisher, book editor, lecturer, lectured, brand strategist, strategy consultant, creative consultant, editorial strategist, creative director, editorial director, founder, co-founder, listicle specialist—as you can understand.

Although my personal employment—or non-employment—history tells of the present economic precarity, it is far from being the core of the argument. Employment, or the lack thereof, does not always and necessarily coincide with identification, as it's often mediated by working relations, bureaucratic structures, and all the external factors that characterize the tasks performed on behalf of, and for, a specific economic entity in the form of "work." Identification has more to do with the word "practice" rather than "work." However, in order for anyone to claim to have a practice, they should have work too. **THE CONUNDRUM OF THE WORK IDENTITY RELATION LIES IN ITS INHERENT NON-LINEARITY**: put simply, not everyone chooses to spell out their job titles as a way to characterize their persona. It is a non-linear construct because a third factor influences its predictability, and that is money.

Axiom A: you work; you earn money.

Axiom B: you work; you earn status (identity currency).

Axiom C: you work; you earn money and status.

How much money? How much status? What money–status ratio? Those are variables that influence the linearity of the work-identity relation, where personal identification with a specific job title might be driven by both types of currencies you earn out of it; or, simply, it might not.

By identification, I mean transferring to mundane activities such as jobs a whole set of cultural values that not only dignify or glorify the work but also build one's personality as an extension of said jobs. This is, paradoxically, a quintessential boomer thinking process that millennials have internalized and made a generational common denominator. If baby boomers lived under the preconception of "work makes me free," obviously opting for money as currency, millennials live under the assumption of "work makes me me," hence opting for status as their currency of choice.

Through all the subaltern categories, outlined above, I've come to impersonate, I've always identified as a writer, although without thinking that activity could contribute as my main source of income, or my core business—rest assured, it wasn't and it is not. Identifying as a writer means, I believe, complying with

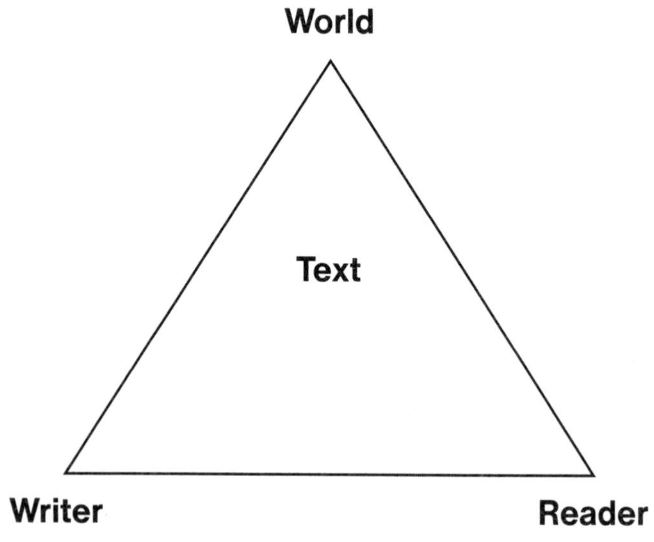

World
Text
Writer
Reader

a methodology of thinking, rather than of doing, to craft ideas that might or might not come to life. Writing today means producing immaterial objects: **CONTEXT MORE THAN CONTENT**. But that shouldn't grant permission to disqualify our profession. Writing is only for pros, because it's such a miserable act that it should never assume the pleasant status of a hobby.

As a kid, I never had the dream of producing any form of writing. No one ever gave me pens and notebooks as encouragement gifts. No words were ever written in a journal in my free time. Teachers wouldn't have me stand up to read my essays in class. I have never read a Harry Potter book in my life. I don't understand poetry, although I was very good at reading ancient Greek back in high school. I never have, and never will embrace the idea of the writer as a naive wordsmith who carries a paperback and pencil tucked in the pockets of a faded, gross work jacket. Am I a good writer? Is my prose reading fine? Are my tenses coordinated? Questions that have never crossed my mind. And to be honest, if they ever did, I would just not care at all.

The mythology of the "street-intellectual" has always been obscured by the perfectly put, publicly acclaimed fake-intellectual. The street-intellectual sells ideas and not words. They sell it to companies, brands, institutions, people, and organizations in the form of condensed, modulated, adaptable language that implies the use of words, but without making it the core of the delivery. Words, for the street-intellectual, are just tools that bear no poetic meaning at all, but are just in service of the thesis, the theory, the *point*. The street-intellectual is a nerd in disguise: someone who's cynical enough to understand their work is not changing the world, but a dreamer at the same time; someone who can talk to a big-company CEO, as much as to an emerging artist, and make their point with the same degree of confidence and conceptual stance; someone who reads but will keep it off the mouth at a club. Someone like a writer, now.

As a true mid, interpretative, derivative,

contemporary writer, I have molded my humble characterization of the street-intellectual on an image that crossed my Google Chrome tab while looking for something else. The image portrays a corny photomontage starring the face of Marshall McLuhan and the body of Tupac. The setting for this mesmerizing visual Frankenstein is a *Rolling Stone* magazine cover, whose headline copy reads: "I am an intellectual thug..." The image couldn't be more fake, although very fitting to the predictions of the media analyst, philosopher, and writer. If for McLuhan, "all media work us over completely," being "so pervasive in their personal, political, economic, aesthetic, psychological, moral, ethical, and social consequences," this image "worked me up" completely too. The original *Rolling Stone* cover story coincides with the death of rapper Tupac Shakur in 1996 at the age of 25—the result of gunshot wounds he had received six days earlier in a drive-by shooting. In the cover portrait, shot by Danny Clinch, Shakur stands still, looking straight at the camera, with his hands crossed behind his back. Shirtless, his torso reveals the iconic "Thug Life" belly tattoo. For Shakur, who decided to replace the letter "I" with a bullet when he got the tattoo in 1992, these two inked words had a duplicitous meaning: the name of the rap group he would found in late 1993, and an acronym for "THE HATE U GIVE LITTLE INFANTS FUCKS EVERYONE," a slogan representing the idea that the racism and marginalization experienced by black youth end up negatively affecting society.

This double-layered writing impressed on Tupac's chest outlines a conceptual framework for the entire lyrical production of the American rapper, in which stratified meanings and different reading keys intertwine one on top of another, making the interpretation of any of his lyrics more complex than their formal delivery. Shakur's complex, deep, emotionally charged writing made him one of the most influential rappers of all time. In 2003, Shakur's impact on contemporary society was the topic of a symposium organized by Harvard University under the title "All Eyez on Me: Tupac Shakur and the Search for a Modern Folk Hero." Among many scholars devoted to furthering the legacy of the rapper into the academic realm, Mark Anthony Neal, currently Professor of African & African American Studies at Duke University, delivered a talk that proposed the reading of Tupac as a politically engaged intellectual, defining him a "thug n**** intellectual." Throughout the panels hosted at the Harvard symposium, Tupac's personal book collection was a recurring topic of discussion, as it emerges from Neal's report debriefing after the event. Included in that collection are books such as J.D. Salinger's *Catcher in the Rye*, Jamaica Kincaid's *At the Bottom of the River*, Herman Melville's classic *Moby Dick*, *Eileen Southern's Music of Black Americans*, and the feminist writings of Alice Walker (*In Search of Our Mother's Gardens*) and Robin Morgan (*Sisterhood is Powerful: Anthology of Writings from the Women's Liberation Movement*). As noted by Neal, "Many of the texts cited above were read before Tupac reached the age of 20."

TUPAC'S TRINOMIAL "READER-WRITER-INTELLECTUAL" DIALECTIC COUNTERBALANCES THE HYPOTHESIS THAT INTELLECTUALS ARE FORMED THROUGH THE SAME PARADIGM OF THE SOCIAL CLASSES,
and overthrows the myth that sees intellectuals as a removed, autonomous, and independent social group. In Antonio Gramsci's *Prison Notebooks*, Vladimir Lenin's infamous declaration that "all distinctions as between workers and intellectuals must be obliterated," is developed in a new, ingenious way by the Italian philosopher, who distinguishes intellectuals into two functional groups. Traditional intellectuals — literary, scientific, ecclesiastic, and so on — whose position in society derives ultimately from past and present class relations and conceals an attachment to historical class formations, and "organic" intellectuals, who act as the thinking and organizing element of a particular fundamental social class. These organic intellectuals are distinguished less

The Hero's Journey
12. Return with Elixir
1. Ordinary World
2. Call to Adventure
3. Refusal of the Call
11. Resurrection
4. Meeting the Mentor
Ordinary World
5. Crossing the Threshold
10. The Road Back
Special World
6. Tests, Allies, Enemies
9. Reward, Seizing the Sword
7. Approach
8. Ordeal, Death, & Rebirth

by their profession, which may be any job characteristic of their class, and more by their ability to shape and influence the ideas and aspirations of the class they organically belong to.

In calling Tupac Shakur an "intellectual thug," Mark Anthony Neal distills Gramsci's idea that the working class, like the bourgeoisie before it, is capable of developing from within its ranks its own organic intellectuals, and that those intellectuals, through their work, represent their class—or, in more modern wording, their community—in society, in public. According to Gramsci, "All men are intellectuals, one could therefore say: but not all men have in society the function of intellectuals," and that, for Gramsci, meant the ideological and political overthrowing of the "Traditional intellectuals" by the hands of the "organic intellectuals." Thug life!

Antonio Gramsci was arrested by the fascist police in 1926, and condemned to a 20-year-long sentence in prison. At his trial, his prosecutor stated, "For twenty years, we must stop this brain from functioning." Other than the brutality of fascist ideology, this statement shows evidence of the role of the intellectual in modern society. This new modality breaks away from the Greco-Roman tradition of the intellectual as a divine repository of knowledge, to characterize the intellectual as an instigator, and in this case, a political opposer, someone whose voice must be silenced and removed from the public sphere: the "organic intellectual." An infamous story published in *Vibe* magazine in 1994 presents Tupac as a menace to society, projecting into the future Gramsci's formulation of a new mode of intellectual activity. "The mode of being of the new intellectual can no longer consist in eloquence, which is an exterior and momentary mover of feelings and passions, but in active participation in practical life, as a constructor, organizer, 'permanent persuader' and not just a simple orator."

If Gramsci was writing these lines from prison from 1929 to 1935, a letter addressed to the British poet Ezra Pound, dated 1951, sent from the office of philosopher and media theorist Marshall McLuhan, once again repurposes the concept of the organic intellectual. "I am an intellectual thug who has been slowly accumulating a private arsenal with every intention of using it. In a mindless age, every insight takes on the character of a lethal weapon. Every man of goodwill is the enemy of society. We prefer to compose human beings into bombs and explode political and social entities. Much more fun."

In terms of being a writer, McLuhan was one of terrible prose. Often described as enigmatic, difficult, and arcane, his writing style employed tight one-liners combined with almost excruciating digressions in historical and literary theory. For McLuhan, who himself defined his "stuff" as "very difficult," his books were just the process, rather than the completed product of discovery. However, over-articulated syntax, convoluted observations, and undecipherable jargon didn't prevent the Canadian philosopher from being widely appreciated by critics as "the high priest of popthink," "the Dr. Spock of pop culture," or "the hottest academic property around." Many others feared him, labeling his theories as dangerous, wrong, and unthinkable. Companies and politicians loved him—General Motors paid him to forecast how cars were a thing of the past, Bell Telephone to have him explain how they were getting the function of the telephone wrong.

A true street-intellectual, McLuhan reshaped society while simultaneously critiquing it. He lived, worked, and thought, on the same surface that was subject to his own interrogations: a true Gramscian intellectual, who chose to identify as a writer for the sole purpose of conveying a message (a massage?). The self-reflexivity of McLuhan's work is of utmost importance, as it provides the paradigm of what it means to produce critical writing today: the writing, simply, must be embedded within society, play by the same rules of contemporary culture, commerce, art, and intellect, to be an effective tool to critique it in turn. Today's short attention

span, algorithmic dissociation, and image hegemony are all pure excuses for writers that aren't pro. If McLuhan managed to put his own name in mainstream media headlines, and build a public persona out of philosophy writing in the heavily illiterate, culture-flattened, mass-brainwashed America of the '60s, while also critiquing these very dynamics, I think we can do it today too.
STREET-INTELLECTUALS ONLY.

CRAZY NARCO-FUELED INVESTOPEDIA

Undiagnosed, Asperger-bending benzodiazepine abuser, psycho-candy loner who walks in silence and cannot cry. Hyphenated agglomeration of words crunched into a single line with no full stop; lack of punctuation, disorganized chaos in decentralized infrastructures. **CLEARLY THE RESULT OF THE HYPERACCELERATION OF HYPEROBJECTS WITH HYPERSTIMULATED UNDERWHELMNESS** that projects nothing else than a desperate what-the-fuck-is-this sort of scenario where I am, most likely, the king.

People talk of the future but I just want to sleep. Sleep, eat, repeat. Cut the "eat," repeat the "sleep."

Detach from the goal, desire nothing. Underachieve, steal everything, forge the dream, rob the happy guy so that he won't keep fucking smiling. "What are you smiling at?" Then carefully proceed to steal the man's wallet. He will keep smiling because he's dumb.

Unemployed doom-blogger angstfluencer death-streamer junkie creepo, you won't invite me to your wedding when you get to marry. I love my followers. I love my people unless they ask me how old I am. Narcissistic toxic behavior is the norm for everyone who understands the above. A bloodstain covers my circularly sourced designer sweatshirt as I murder my integrity walking out of a party I wasn't invited to and was promptly rejected from. Invest in ethical bonds; invest in off-the-radar crypto; invest in emerging markets; invest in sustainable clothing; invest in auto-generated literature and journalism; invest in content farms; invest in dissociative drugs; invest in emerging startups connecting talent with employers;

INVEST IN ANYTHING OUTSIDE YOURSELF AND YOU'LL BE FINE.

Products I like ranked in no particular order, divided by semicolons for clarity's sake: LinkedIn; orange juice; fake fur; followers; chargers and power banks of any type; semicolons; pencils; turtlenecks; Loro Piana; the Sochi Winter Olympics mascots:

the Hare, the Polar Bear, and the Leopard, respectively created by Silviya Petrova, Oleg Seredechniy, and Vadim Pak; .mp3 files; lace nightgowns; associative logic; the Dot-com bubble; murder cases from the '70s; the early-2020s Google Maps interface; listicles; family money.

He (A) was carrying home a package they had bought from their own company—a tech start-up mapping mood-regulatory drug intake, offering personalized drug diets, and connecting users with sellers of such drugs. A true marketplace for the future. The courier refused to deliver the parcel to the door as it appeared poorly packaged—each seller distributes the parcels on their own terms, HEAVEN-X has no liability for the exchange whatsoever—taped with fluorescent hazard-sign stickers in an indistinguishable foreign alphabet, so he had to carry the burden from the ground to the eleventh floor. Everyone in the building's lobby just stared at the object in awe and terror, doorman included. The otherwise-ordinary scene was now fed with extreme anticipation and mystery. Voices from every corner of the building triumphed in an unwelcomed symphony of democratic speculations while the main character was fatiguing to bring the goofily packaged article home. "6, 5, 4, 3, 2, 1, 0–Lobby," doors open, item slides, orientation flipped off 90 degrees to maximize space for body; doors close; eleventh floor reached; ding dong.

B: "Sorry, didn't hear the courier buzzing. I could have helped with... what IS that?"
A: "Don't worry about that."
B: "It looks like shit."
A: "It's just like Amazon."
B: "Okay, then, shall we?"
A: "Terrace?"
B: "What if it's a scam?"
A: "Oh, well, I don't think they accept returns, you know..."
B: "I figured. And who is 'they,' exactly?"
A: "Terrace!"
Products I don't like, ranked in no particular order, divided by semicolons for clarity's sake: irony; suicides taking place in the midst

of a Zoom call; flannel shirts; Tumblr; cinema; water; country-specific plug and socket types; paved streets; two football teams competing for a minor-league trophy; blue-ink pens; plan Bs; Oscar fucking Wilde; investigative journalism; remarkably small and elongated wine glasses; the 1967 concept album *Sgt. Pepper's Lonely Hearts Club Band*; interactive service totems; graphic design; the Seattle 1962 World Expo fair—the first appearance of the IBM Shoebox.

Approximately 32 sqm—fenced by an iron and concrete handrail, paved in greige squared tiles, and overlooked by a retractable PVC tent—divide the house from the rest of the sky. A set of 12 narrow steps leads to an upstairs terraced space that precedes the building's "official" roof. This bootlegged, unofficial roof-looking esplanade is secluded from the gaze of neighbors, and it's almost logically attached to the house as its conditions of access (the stairs) are embedded within the allocated portion of the private residence. Air and atmospheric agents are perhaps the only others in the know of this architectural secret.

Downstairs, a plastic table and garden-ish furniture are stacked onto the left side of the private terrace, looking long-lasting and disposable at the same time.

The terrace-home complex sits on a rectangular stretch of the eleventh floor of a building in an undisclosed location of a pathologically ill urban segment whose inhabitants label "city." Inside, no carpets are allowed—not for science but for style. No earth tones; no colors at all. No wood; no cotton. Desks, more desks, and other desk-looking objects are placed strategically around the house with performative casualness.

B: "It's cold out here."
A: "Where is my phone?"
B: "I think we should go out more often."
A: "My phone..."
B: "What?"
A: "I need to check my numbers."
B: "You're rich, chill out."
A: "Not those numbers."
B: "Which numbers?"
A: "MY numbers."

In therapy, I have been called the following, ranked in no particular order, divided by semicolons for clarity's sake: patient; bipolar; psychotic; person; dear; symptomatic; neglected; almost ready; fully functioning; improving; individual; archetype; obsessive; a; fucking; addictive; personality. Up-and-down-and-up-and-down-and-up-and-down swings.

[Push notifications allowed]

"This is Ω, your HEAVEN-X mentor. It's October 19, 2049 and your drug intake has lowered by 13%. Consider refueling." Bzz-Bzz-Bzzzzzz-Bzz-Bzz. "HEAVEN-X Mood Report—Serotonin: 48% down. Dopamine: 78% down. Norepinephrine: 53% down. Endorphin: 44% down. Consider refueling."

B: "What now? Tweet your numbers?"
A: "No. I recalibrate."
B: "Until?"
A: "Until the numbers look good."
B: "It really can get out of hand."
A: "What couldn't?"

B: "Excuse me?"
A: "What could not get out of hand?
As in, I am out of hand, you are out of hand,
everything is out of hand."
B: "That's not the reason to just keep millions
of users hooked on drugs."
A: "On the app, we're just data."
B: "And off the app?"
A: "I don't know."
B: "We're just addicts."
A: **"WE'RE JUST HEAVEN-X CLIENTS."**
B: "A community, LOL…"

No glory, no fame, no affection—I am a result
of corporate angst and service industrialism. A
venture capitalist of the abyss, an angel investor
in the sense that I am Lucifer, fell from heav-
en, absorbed by this surprisingly miserable
gathering of words, thoughts, and flesh. This
year alone, the global population amounted to
twenty-three billion two hundred fifty-nine
million terabytes (23.259.000000). Data are
still the most profitable asset since the 2030s.
Global, dispersed boredom; an IPO for your
life; a formulaic gesture.

A: "It's time."

B: "Let me finish... we always said HEAVEN-X was ethically unethical."

A: "I don't have time to be corporate-vision lectured now."

B: "You're a slave to your own company."

A: "My numbers just need to look good."

B: "Do they also feel good?"

A: "Let's open the package and I'll tell you."

B: "And then? Every package means a new life? A new start? A new mood?"

A: "A new week for sure."

B: "It's scary."

A: "No big deal. We're not saving lives here."

B: "We're definitely not."

Things people want to do before they commit suicide, ranked in no particular order, divided by semicolons for clarity's sake: say goodbye to their family and loved ones; affirm themselves for the last time; get laid; affirm themselves for the first time; mindmap the aftermath; shoot heroin; nothing; think about the idealized image of themselves. HEAVEN-X can help.

A NEW WAY
FOR THE
OLD GAME!

Invest in tiny houses; invest in the ketamine industry; invest in the luxury fashion monogroup monopoly; invest in iceberg restoration; invest in lab-generated diamonds; invest in tech start-ups connecting diagnosed individuals with the drug market.

[Phone buzz]

"Dear A,

On the occasion of Men's Fashion Week in October 2049, HEAVEN-X is delighted to invite you to the opening of CATHEDRAL, a new cultural center building and nurturing a culturally conscious, new-generation audience in the world's fashion and design capital. CATHEDRAL is a social space where art, design, and fashion blend to shape new cultural experiences, hosted in a former industrial building of over 1000 square meters. Originating from the vision of visionary founding partner HEAVEN-X, the space will open in October 2049.
RSVP is required: rsvp@heaven-x.com

Warmly,

Ω,
your HEAVEN-X mentor."

A HOUSE IN THE MOUNTAINS
(INTERLUDE)

We avoid mediocrity by acknowledging how our lives—simple lives—can drift away from what's normal just by following what our hearts tell us. This makes us special, makes us alive, makes us happy. **HAPPINESS, FUCK THAT, WAS NEVER IN THE PICTURE**. But what was in the picture was instinct, *guts*. My family has only lived by the way of guts. And so did I, together with them. Choosing what our hearts told us was never a luxury, a privilege, a naivety; but a need, a condition, a fact.

Small family, mine. Only children gave birth to more only children. Middle-class relationships gave birth to middle-class altercations. Middle-class altercations gave birth to middle-class years of silence. And that gave birth to more years of middle-class silence. And that, together with life, people, and death, gave birth to a smaller family. Mine.

Fifty percent of my family traveled. Away. To South America, to Venezuela, settled for a bit, to Philadelphia, settled for good. Offspring are born. And our house in the mountains is still there. Where everybody came from. Where my mother was born. Where my grandad shoveled dirt in order to make a garden for all of us.

All of us, we are just two. Two only-children-cousins born out of exhausted small circles of people that Italians dare to call families. The clichè of that big-ass, loud-ass, love-ass family is definitely not ours. And, not mine. The House in the Mountains could house more family members than the ones we really ended up with. The House in the Mountains was seen by more people than the ones that have actually ever seen it. I just know that a commercial spot showcasing the House was aired in local cinemas in between movie trailers. In the '70s. The guts. An act of my grandad—a hustler, an accidental ad-man—who I've had barely the privilege of meeting before his self-inflicted baroque passing. We avoid mediocrity by acknowledging how our lives can drift away from what's normal just by following what our hearts tell us.

And here I am, giving advice on style, aesthetics, sociology, semiotics, luxury items, mass-disseminated items (I don't care), tangible things, intangible things, behaviors, objects, shoes, t-shirts, pants, socks, paintings, sculptures, installations—and I couldn't care less. The only thing I care about is my House in the Mountains, and its unfaithful destiny. The fact that it's on sale because of a family mismanagement. Because it answers to the negligence of generations, although unpopulated, but alive. Including myself. And the answer I would love to give to the house is just: "Let me buy you back." Have you ever read your name spelled wrong? The lady at the general register office, when I was born, made me and my dad a huge favor: a new dynasty born out of mundane misinterpretation and lack of culturally accepted education. One letter, one different legacy. **A TYPO???** But guess what, I am, now, so happy. Not for the name but for the story it upholds—a product of honest resilience. For the people who don't empathize: a brand-new last name, in rural Italy, is an object of question, is a matter of scrutiny, is a field of analysis, is the driver of many questions: Who are you the son of?

We avoid mediocrity by acknowledging what our hearts tell us. I was born with a pure heart and you can't say the opposite. Everyone in my family was born with a pure heart and that's our fucking disgrace. Pure like white. Pure like virgin. Pure like unedited. Pure like a choice: be humble, stay pure. I don't know if I manage to stand by that today. But still, like the House, I'm here because of the guts. I'm here not for the luxury, but for the need. Like the House, I'm here because people were before me, here. And I'm fucking here too.

NOTES ON HI-VIS

British police in reflective-striped neon jackets annihilating Brexit protesters. Fluorescent-clothed emergency workers responding to the Coronavirus pandemic. An army of yellow vests sabotaging the French establishment. A safety yellow Arc'teryx anorak layered over bridal tulle in Off White's Fall Winter 2020 runway show. In the following few months, if you had access to the media landscape in any possible way, these images likely stuck in your mind, hardly forgettable as the textiles in them have been devised for maximum retinal stimulation. Recently, there's been a boost of high-visibility garments, both in fashion and news images, shifting the subtext of how we interpret signifiers of both safety and luxury. By mimesis, high-visibility dissimulates the tropes of protest, the working class, surveillance, authority, and emergency — and by appropriation, it responds to growing discomfort with the capitalist framework, which its critique is also sometimes subsumed by.

While workwear is a product of the Industrial Revolution, high-visibility workwear is indeed a more recent invention, dating back to the 1930s. At the time, workers unions were gaining recognition and political influence, especially in the US, demanding expanded workplace health and safety measures while labor regulations were beginning to be applied more consistently. In 1930 in Berkeley, California, Bob Switzer suffered a coma, following a workplace accident unloading crates at a railroad yard. Following doctor's orders to stay in a dark room while he recovered, Switzer started experimenting with chemicals that had fluorescent effects, leading to eventually, together with his brother Joe, developing a paint they called Day-Glo. Once applied, Day-Glo made materials shine brightly as if it were daylight even in the dark. The brothers, who were also amateur magicians, first used the paint to achieve optical illusions for their stage acts, but the US military soon took an interest. It was WWII and the army saw the potential for this new technology to help identify troops to aircrafts overhead, thereby preventing friendly-fire casualties. They prompted the Switzer brothers to start experimenting with applying the fluorescent pigments to fabrics. By the 1960s, uniforms embedded with fluorescent paneling, and the Day-Glo Fire Orange™, became the standard of safety in aviation.

Hi-vis became more and more ubiquitous, growing into a globally acknowledged signifier of risk and safety, used not only in the military but also by construction workers, crossing guards, police officers, toll gate personnel, and frontline workers. **IT'S A SHORT JUMP FROM SAFETY TO EMERGENCY.** In a natural disaster, pandemic, civil unrest, or armed conflict — situations where a government can declare a state of emergency and curtail civilian rights — there's increased demand for hi-vis fluorescent and reflective materials, communicating emergent hazards and alerting people to changes in protocol. Italian philosopher Giorgio Agamben situates the state of emergency at an "ambiguous and uncertain fringe at the intersection of the legal and the political," constituting a "point of disequilibrium between public law and political fact." Under those circumstances, democracy is potentially under threat of hijacking.

After the 9/11 terrorist attacks, then President George W. Bush declared a state of emergency, which he used to rationalize programs of wiretapping and torture as well as military operations in Iraq and Afghanistan. In this post-Department of Homeland Security era, military hi-vis gained greater notoriety in the public imagination.

Around the mid-2000s, the glow belt became especially iconic, with images from Iraq and Afghanistan showing US troops wearing these reflective belts everywhere, during physical training, walking at night, operating all-terrain vehicles, even as a pass of sorts to get into the chow hall. These belts shaped the visual narrative of the War on Terrorism, to the point that their renown crossed over into civilian fashion. In 2018, Urban Outfitters started selling their own $30 "Rothco Reflective Physical Training Belt." The reflective belt had been established as the true icon of the state of emergency.

As the concept of democracy mutates within the post-factual realm, a univocal definition of emergency is no longer applicable.

The 2016 US presidential election, populist movements gaining government majority in Italy, the recent right-wing coup of the Hungarian Parliament, and the *gilets jaunes* in France exemplify how the rise of social media has paved the way for autonomous movements to gain the status of recognized political forces, engineering a crowd-sourced legitimation process for radical ideas. Through audience fragmentation and behaviorally targeted content, "the people" grew into an identifiable political entity with an anti-elite agenda. As protests around the world are on the rise, one thing is certain: today the state of emergency can be the act of a bottom-up declaration, one that is claimed upon the establishment.

In October 2018, nearly every newspaper around the world would publish an image featuring hi-vis yellow vests. The movement of the *gilets jaunes* in France is a top-of-the-iceberg manifestation of a new state of emergency, one that is crowd-deliberated and perpetrated through public violence. The *gilets jaunes* have no established leaders,

no clear aims, and few unifying characteristics, though the movement's adherents
all seem to find a common ground on their
dress code: the fluorescent yellow hazard
vest that has become synonymous with the
French working class's outcry over fuel taxes.
"There hasn't been such a compelling sarto-
rial symbol of revolt since the Sans-culottes
seized on their trousers as the point of visual
difference with the aristocracy during the
French Revolution, " writes *The New York
Times* fashion critic Vanessa Friedman. The
gilets jaunes movement understands that
**IN OUR IMAGE-CENTRIC CULTURE, TO BE
HEARD YOU HAVE TO BE SEEN.**

Prior to the *gilets jaunes* taking to the
streets, hi-vis gear had been showing up in
music videos and streetwear collections—
from Yung Lean's video for "Kyoto" in 2013
to Heron Preston's collaboration with the
New York Department of Sanitation. The
popularity of neon orange, neon yellow, and
3M reflective materials seemed an offshoot
of the construction workwear trend which
itself had been identified as a variation on

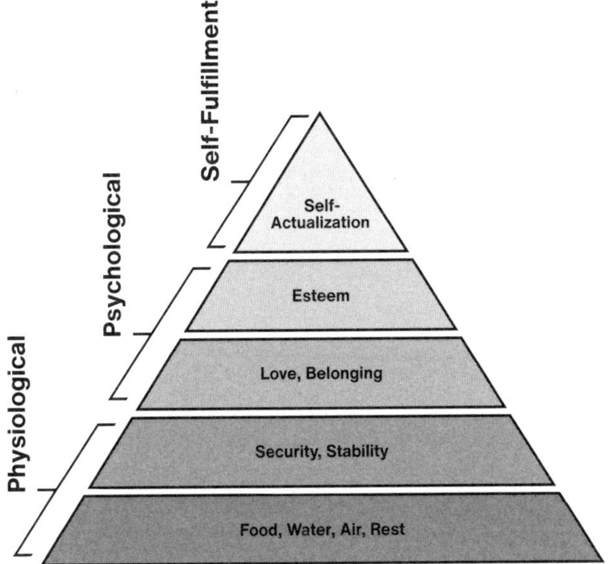

Self-Fulfillment
Psychological
Physiological
Self-Actualization
Esteem
Love, Belonging
Security, Stability
Food, Water, Air, Rest

the normcore phenomenon from a few years prior—yet another cycle of self-aware appropriation, this one evoking hazard assessment and utilitarian safety.

Luxury fashion caught up on the safety gear trend pretty quickly, and the Fall 2018 runway shows acted as self-fulfilling prophecies for the *gilets jaunes* protests to come a few months later. Calvin Klein's (205W39NYC) ready-to-wear collection delivered hi-vis stripes, plastic gloves, fireman-inspired rubber boots, and metallic survival blankets styled to accessorize similarly silver dresses. If Raf Simons had been reading Agamben, he wasn't the only one. That same year, a highlighter-orange coat made an appearance at Burberry's runway show, and Junya Watanabe's collection took its inspiration from the uniforms of firefighters, police officers, mail carriers, and sanitation workers — almost every piece with a reflective band.

After it was embraced by luxury brands and the fashion establishment, hi-vis infiltrated mainstream consumerism with fast-fashion brands releasing an overabundance of neon pieces, with the media marketing the eye-catching trend as self-expression and a "buzzing" antidote to a lack of confidence. The Kardashian-Wests were early-adopters — **KIM EVEN MATCHED NEON OUTFITS WITH HER NEON YELLOW MERCEDES SUV** — their trendsetting eventually spawning an army of Instagram influencers in highlighter-hued sweatshirts.

Just as the *gilets jaunes* suggest a decentralization of emergency, the circulation of neon fashions in some ways challenges the expected top-down path from luxury to fast fashion. Balenciaga — a brand well-versed in post-ironic appropriation at the weird intersection of Reddit theory and Austro-Hungarian aristocracy costume — first introduced fluorescent hues in their Spring Summer 2017 ready-to-wear collection: instant classics like the spandex stocking-boots appeared in neon yellow, hi-orange, and shocking pink. But as hi-vis was embraced by Instagram influencers and fast-fashion brands, Balenciaga didn't shy away. Instead, through best-selling items like the World Food tops or the *Triple-S*, the house carried on the hi-vis trend, acknowledging the situational power of luxury when it comes to representing authority in mass-culture. The luxurification of emergency in Balenciaga is of no less importance than the politicization of emergency discussed above — in this process, citizens equal customers and populism extends its definition to top-tier price tags.

Psycho-effective hues are absorbed and represented by visual culture as signifiers for a hyper-accelerated political context, and the new state of emergency becomes a direct response to the new state of anxiety. According to Maslow's hierarchy of needs, safety needs are considered foundational, second only to physiological needs like air, water, food, shelter, etc. In the current scenario of existential turbulence — when "stay safe" has become the default valediction and safety has been increasingly revealed as a luxury — we can't help but strategize coping mechanisms to reconnect to the self, address the brutality of the neoliberal day-to-day, and strive for visibility in systems that overlook our humanity. But should this process be exploited for a fashion brand's bottom line, or a micro-influencer's social clout? A millennial, fashion-woke version of the *gilets jaunes* is the last thing we need.

DEAR DIARY BENZO (FREESTYLE)

I'm not even typing this one. I'm handwriting it. For work, I've mused on art, music, fashion, style, and the politics of it all. I've mused on people, and eventually, they became my people. I've worked with ideas, I've worked with things. I've loved ideas, I've loved things. I've loved people too.

An agreement. That's what you sign. When you sign on to me. I'm mafia. I'm a suburban law firm. I'm a subprime credit default swap broker. I'm an institutional loan. I'm a fucking BANK! When it comes to friendship. Negative aspects, one might think. I dare. Contracts are everywhere. And you have to be fucking stupid not to understand that. You subscribe to Netflix as much as you subscribe to a friendship. Or, at least, a real one. The only thing is, although Netflix gives you company when you need it—just like a friend—you can't be fake to Netflix. You can't cap with Netflix. Because it removes your friendship as soon as you stop committing to it (or, well, paying for it). Are you still watching?... I'm on a Netflix agenda right now. Modus operandi: fake-friend corporate downsizer; reverse HR recruiting; divorce lawyer procedure. **UNSUBSCRIBE. DISMISS. UNFOLLOW. DISENGAGE.** I've learned the meaning of the word "bro" only in the context of friendship. I've never used the word "bro" outside the context of friendship. Only child. And wild. We're disgustingly different. We all must meet our "Moment of Truth." You hear me. Instead of Gang Starr, we're gang-fucked. My friends are my subculture, and I exist within the codes and the structures that it posits. My fake friends are my subculture, and I'm game within the codes and the structure it posits. Favors, numbers, names, books, cash, presence, services, words, attention, legitimacy, clout, inspiration, motivation, reassurance, attention, ideas, energy, commitment, meals, beers, wines, sofas, beds, drugs, music, introductions, tips, intelligence, insights, gossip, banter, weekends, time—a lot of time—that's what you ask. And you don't know until you find out.

Sometimes I imagine a world without me. Which is fine. Problem is, I keep stuff. I keep things, inanimate and animate. Things, and people. I have an extremely addictive personality and that reflects tout court in everything I do, love, buy, and live. Tout court. Tout-the-fucking-court. You gotta run with the ball, tout court. I don't want my legacy in the world to be fake friends. Or fake words. I keep things because things are easier to manage. I keep books, records, memorabilia, notebooks, handwritten Post-it notes, old phones, and Macbooks. Easier companions.

IT'S ALL SLIME-SLIME UNTIL THINGS GO LIFE-LIFE.

Work friends: The worst. Case-A fakes. Employer-friend: even worse. Class-A abusers. I'm not really in the business of mingling. Nor in that of pleasing. Or in that of clout-bombing, or ping-pong-tagging, or Escher-reposting.

(With respect to "Escher-reposting," I mean a tendency that's over-abused on the social media platform of Instagram, where stories are reposted in an endless tunnel of refraction of the same piece of content that's shared and re-shared by the two tagged counterparts until it formally shows up as an optical illusion in which the original image has been ping-ponged so many times between the two stakeholders that it becomes an illusion—an Escher-esque optical illusion—in which **THE MEANING IS LOST THROUGH THE PROCESS, BUT ATTENTION IS MAXIMIZED.** At what stake, I might ask. At the stake of seeming fucking ridiculous, not just for the desperation behind this act, but because the original content is lost and its impact is diminished by the two actors' egos. In this gesture, capitalizing on ego might maximize attention, but it minimizes the core product—namely, here, a picture shared on some Instagram story—that's bigger originally, but made smaller proportionally to the number of re-shares the two accounts agree on.)

Fuck ego. Fuck optical illusions. And fuck Escher too.

Benzodiazepines are kicking in. There's a trend on TikTok where girls ask their boyfriends how much they think about the Roman Empire. I think this has to do with masculinity and alpha behavior. Especially if looked at from a North American perspective. I, for example, have answered that question. I said that I think about it every month, or more.

What if we played "dear-diary?"

Dear Diary, here I am *not* in my childhood bedroom writing in my diary. I know you're only a simple, Western-derivative literary device. Dear fucking diary, I am writing and I am not writing in a diary. I am writing for how much I am able to communicate. For how much I am able to verbalize. For how much I am able to expose feelings. To friends, fake and real. I'd rather fill this stupid diary with "heys," or hey-sounding phonemes; adlibs to some verses that no one cares about. Matter of fact, I'd rather be talking to my friends, the ones who are still around me at least. The ones who will read this and smile and will be happy for me, as I would.

Fake friends, *faux amis*. In English grammar, it means "a word in a different language that looks or sounds similar to a word in a given language, but differs significantly in meaning." Fake friends, sneaky friends. English "embarrassed" and Spanish "embarazada" (for pregnant) is a common example. You avoid fake friends. That's why they're called such.

It's all slime-slime until things go life-life. Until clients become client-clients. Until clout becomes your-your clout. Until professional autonomy becomes *"automatic No!"* Until passive aggressive becomes the past. Until work emails become my emails. Until people who called me family will keep ignoring my work. Until people who called me family could dig no more; exploit no more; exhaust no more. Until 9-to-5 became 9-to-5-to-6-back-to-9. But it doesn't matter, at least there are no fake friends involved.

PROLETARIAN DRIFT

We progress class by imitation, and we digress by appropriation. We move upwards by aspiration, we move downwards by pathetic simulation. We absorb to dissimulate. We analyze to steal. We borrow, and we return on our terms. We climb up, and we climb backwards. Depending on who we are, of course. It requires the same effort to either downgrade or upgrade, the effort in question being a weirdly humane combination of willingness, self-awareness, and benchmarking capability. We go up, and we go down. We upscale, and we downscale. We are not all the same "we."

THIS IS GETTING BINARY, AND AS MUCH AS I'D LOVE TO MAKE IT DIFFERENT, CLASS IS SOMETHING—PERHAPS THE ONLY THING—YOU CAN'T QUEER.

As a matter of fact, class is a real construct, and it manifests across the entire spectrum of society. Anything you think, want, and do is somehow related to your class—whether the class you're born in or the class you aspire to. Mobility between different classes is possible, and more and more frequent. But when the transfer is accomplished, you still carry the values and the identity pillars that formed within your place of origin in the class system. There's beauty in this, but you still have to deal with the implications.

Class drifting is an act of transition between different, and sometimes opposite, systems of value. Whether it's upwards or downwards is irrelevant: it's still a mobility paradigm. There are two ends of the spectrum, as there always will be. High and Low. As binary as it gets, this system is, by nature, fixed until you break it. How? Just drift it. *Skk-skk-skk.*

Many theorists have tried to deconstruct, or contextualize, the movements and implications of class, although adhering to the standards of form and delivery that it demanded. Writing philosophy in the 19th century, although philosophy about the proletarian class, demanded a formalization that differed from its subject. Put simply: you can't write an academic paper about someone who can't read. The flaws in the European post-structuralist movement unfold the path to an unexplored territory of class fermentation. The subject is long forgotten because predatorily exploited by many who didn't manage to translate the essence of class struggle into the real world. In the post-Marxist deconstructivist legacy of Habermas, Baudrillard, Adorno, Foucault, Gramsci, Deleuze, and Guattari—although some are more compelling than others—words are lost within language, and ideas are lost within words.

Today, talking about class bears a certain weight. What is still certain: you can drift along.

If the concept of class was so monolithic that it needed to be deconstructed, today it is so deconstructed that it has to be monolithized. The discourse around class needs a reset. The discourse around class needs disillusionment, as much as irony. We must pick up on the same agenda of our post-Marxist weirdo predecessors and bring the discourse into the current arena. One way to do so is, of course, going back to classic texts and trying to carefully extract meaning without mystifying the original meaning and getting caught in the trap of its originators.

Drifting away from pre-war Continental philosophy, America picks up with class studies in the aftermath of the economic boom of the 1960s. The topic is mostly discussed across academic networks, within faculties like Anthropology and Sociology. In the UK, Raymond Williams—perhaps the only valid class scholar of modernity who escaped the hegemony of the text in favor of its content—postulates his coinage of "cultural materialism" in the early 1960s. While these people write about class, the citizens of the Western world buy stuff—a lot of stuff—and sign mortgages for property, for cars, for status purchases, for watches, for cruises, for Concorde air miles, for credit card debt, for cash. That's the era of assets before income, the era of "I want it" before "I can afford it." That's the era of class drift. And that era lasted until the 2000s.

In 1983, Paul Fussell wrote about the American class system with great clarity and insightful wit. In his book *Class*, he eviscerated the canons, styles, and codes of the social classes, filtered through an exquisitely observant point of view. Fussell is still a majorly overlooked figure today, although his cultural criticism offered a sharp interpretation of the mechanisms of class construction: through objects, attitudes, symbols, myths, and styles. A genius, in my opinion—or at least a good writer.

Class: A Guide Through the American Status System is a very simple book. It is a book that talks about society from lifestyle optics; it is a book that is meant to be read; it is a book that tells a story rather than telling the truth; it is a book that forges critical analysis in its readers. In the book, he says, you're either an Upper-Class, an Upper-Middle, a Middle, a High Prole, or a Mid- or Low-Prole. There's no escape. And in his book it makes sense. But today, although enlightening, it really doesn't matter.

What I see today is rich people going *prolewards* for the sake of grounding themselves in the world. Rich guys want to be part of our world, *the* world, and they try their best to make themselves accustomed to our vernacular. Birkenstocks are an entry point to wholesome styling: your LVMH-owned friendly neighbor who always smiles in the hallway. I get it; if I were rich, I would probably behave that way—the opposite of Fussell's Upper-Class portrayal—I would be trying my best to look like us, like *me*. I would sink class, and not just sink, but I would sink *successfully*. I would not only impersonate, but I would empathize. I would resonate with the values. I would echo the reason why. I would dissect the stigma. I would pick up the codes. I would absorb the milieu. I would behave like I was. I would move, just, prolewards! If only I had been born rich, I would have understood.

To sink successfully: a practice for the elite. No one masters this particular skill outside of the very chosen few who were blessed to be born rich but deemed to behave poor. By sinking, they paradoxically acquire status, while on the opposite side, hustlers try to get a lift up the very same ladder. This is very simplistic, but, once again, I wasn't born rich.

What I was born is, among other things, curious. And that's why I've known many rich, many middle, and many prole people. And still today I can only relate to one group among them. What do the others do?

Prolewards! Sink successfully into a glass of wine that's been harvested within a mile radius and incorporates holy particles gravitating around a somehow sacred atmosphere surrounding a discarded vineyard in the south of Sicily. Sink successfully into an organic lifestyle reminiscent of parent's bank accounts and olive oil trees. Sink successfully into post-boho-online-beatnik lifestyles, like smoking pot with Seth Rogen-designed paraphernalia or simply wearing mountain clothes in social urban contexts. Sink successfully! Prolewards! You're empowered and naturally sinking classes. Organically sinking. Like a bathtub that needs a hydraulic intervention. You sink.

You're drifting class. You're prole drifting. *Skk-skk-skk.* Congratulations! You have to downgrade. You have to... look poor. It's amazing how this simple dynamic has transcended the societal imperative of "radical chic" to become normalized. The rich today have to sink even more than that. For Tom Wolfe, "radical chic" was a sort of a catch-all umbrella term to define any individual of the upper class who would intentionally downgrade to the manners of the beat youth for the sake of social acceptance. This is extremely different today because "society"—which, at the time of Wolfe's writing, meant fundraising dinners in fancy Upper East Side penthouses—is not happening behind closed doors anymore. Today, to sink means to commit.

And you're committed to that. You sink so good. You sink while we rise. You go prolewards, we go lifewards. *Prolewards!* That's where we're going, like if you got me in an Uber and picked the destination in advance. *Prolewards!* We're going where this random Sorbonne–NYU–CSM–Goldsmiths student is taking us. *Prolewards!* I'll have what they're having. *Prolewards!* Where university exams become reality and the Habermas–Baudrillard–Adorno–Foucault–Gramsci–Deleuze—

Guattari dream team queues up for retirement checks. *Prolewards!* I love to be here. It's the journey, not the destination:

Prolewards!

Damn, boy, I wish.

At this point, you might be questioning whether your status is among the rich or the poor. At the end of the day, the response, for my generation, is to be found only within your inherited wealth. Attitude plays a big deal in this equation, no matter the philosophy you pretend you read or the habits you develop in society. People will always be reflected by their economic status because that's the most precise, imminent, punctual portrayal of the self. No matter your blue eyes or your perfect nose, you will always have to deal with your money—none or many.

Where I want to go with this essay, I don't exactly know. I just know I feel the urgency to, first, dissociate myself from whatever snobby, academic, post-Marxist intelligentsia, and I think I managed so far. Then it comes to the "organic" idealists: I hate you so much; you should try and live one single day in the city where I was born. Then it goes for the Instagram leftists, to whom I remind that being poor, for someone else, is not an option, like for yourself. *Prolewards!*

Where I want to go with this essay is definitely not prolewards. I have been prole, and I am going towards. *Skk-skk-skk.* I'm drifting upwards, for a change, because it's the only place where fake people are not allowed. *Skk-skk-skk.* You're sinking. Sinking successfully. Because that's what your parents didn't mean for you. While you *natural whine*, I *natural win.* And with me, many like me.

Thank you for reading my book.

THE LIVING ROOM SCALE (BONUS TRACK)

Revised (Twice)

(An early, primitive form of this was promulgated in 1935 by F. Stuart Chapin in his book *Contemporary American Institutions*)

(A more recent adaptation of this—as well as an inspiration for my version—was published in 1983 as the appendix of Class. A Guide Through the American Status System by Paul Fussell.)

In this current version, the questionnaire's score results are recalibrated and adapted to the present spectrum of attitudes, revisiting Fussell's taxonomy that was based on class and wealth, at a time in which the dependency between these was undoubtedly more linear.

Instructions:
Begin with a score of 100. For each of the following items present in your living room (and/or office space, or studio) add or subtract points as indicated. Then ascertain social class according to the table at the end.

Pre-2000 IKEA	(+3)
Natural wine fair poster	(-2)
Virgil Abloh: Figures of Speech book	(-1)
Virgil Abloh: Figures of Speech book (collector's edition)	(-5)
Virgil Abloh: Figures of Speech book (sent directly by the author)	(+5)
Porcelain incense holder	(+2)
Wooden incense holder	(-1)
Shoe boxes, visible	(-4)
Drugs station	(+8)
Aluminum snorting straws	(+4)
Ashtrays	(+4)
Any item exhibiting words in an ancient or modern foreign language (German preferred. Spanish excluded.)	(+7 each)
Bicycle kept in the living room	(-3)
Flags. Of any kind	(-8)
Alexa	(-2)

Furniture designed by yourself   (+3 each)
Stussy sofa blanket   (+2)
Kartell "Componibili"   (-1)
Stairs   (+8)
Stairs, for bookshelf   (+9)
No-shoe policy on the sofa   (-1)
iMac used as TV screen   (-2)
Two sofas   (+2)
Two objectively cool sofas   (+4)
Anything "Eames"   (-1)
Anything Japanese   (+2 each)
Magazines visible:

    Monocle   (+1)
    032c   (+3)
    The Paris Review   (+5)
    Buffalo   (+2)
    Texte Zur Kunst   (+10)
    Artforum   (+2)
    FlashArt   (-2)
    Apartamento   (+1)
    Dazed   (-2)
    Arena Homme+   (+2)
    System   (+3)
    Purple   (+1)
    Frieze   (-2)

Interview	(+2)
The Wire	(+4)
i-D	(-2)
Parquet floor	(+8)
Resin floor	(+3)
Gres porcelain floor	(-1)
Fake-wood linoleum	(-3)
Vitsoe wall-to-wall bookshelf	(+3)
Terrarium and/or aquarium	(-3)
Any wall-to-wall bookshelf filled with books	(+8)
Macbook	(+1 each)
Phone with cover	(-1)
Anything from Tekla	(+3)
Diptyque candle	(-1)
You bought the living room	(+6)
Floor-to-ceiling windows	(+5 each)
Conversation pit	(+9)
Any item indicating your name or initials	(-3)
An object you inherited	(+2 each)
You inherited the living room	(+3)
Magnets of any kind	(-2)
Stickers of any kind	(-1)
Blackboard and chalk	(-3)

Day-bed   (+3)
Anything Sottsass and/or Ponti   (+5 each)
Empty bottles of natural wine
    on display   (-2)
Empty bottles of natural wine used
    as candle holders   (-4)
Kuumba incense   (+2)
Anything signed by someone famous   (-2)
Anything signed by someone famous,
    framed   (-3)
Art signed by a practicing,
    legit artist. Dead or alive.   (+4 each)
Enough chairs for a dinner party   (+4)
Coins everywhere   (-2)
JBL portable speaker   (-3)
Projector   (-1)
A proper coat rack   (+2)
Any collectible homeware ever
    posted on Hypebeast   (-5)
Liquor/bar cart   (+3)
Trestle table   (-1)
Artifacts from Islands.
    Any island.   (+5 each)
Real flowers in real vases   (+1)
Playstation and/or XBox   (-3)

Live-laugh-love items, displayed
    ironically (+5)
Tabletop of marble or glass (+9)
Books stacked all over the place (+6)
Glassdoor to terrace/balcony (+5)
Spotify with ads (-2)
IG blue tick. Paid (-8)
Tidal Pro (+2)
Apple Music (+3)
Spotify family. Your family pays (-3)
Spotify family. You pay for your
    family (+6)
Coffee table in marble and/or glass (+3)
Cleaning supplies and tools are
    hidden in a storage closet (+2)
Kitchen is in the living room (-2)
Living room is in the kitchen (-4)
Each piece of design over
    30 years old (+2 each)
Each piece of design bought
    straight from the store (+3 each)
Fireplace (+10)
Second floor or above (+2)
First floor (+1)
Ground floor (-1)

Books laying on your coffee table:
  Amalfi (or any other location)
  Assouline Books   (-5 each)
  Yayoi Kusama x Louis Vuitton book (-4)
  Entryways of Milan   (-3)
  Prada (or any other brand)
    Catwalk book   (-2 each)
  Stone Island: Storia Revised and
    Updated   (-1)
  Wolfgang Tillmans. Four Books   (+1)
  S, M, L, XL: OMA   (+2)
  Any Fondazione Prada
    catalogue   (+3 each)
  Any book purchased on
    Idea Books "superbooks"
    section   (+4 each)
  Financial reports and/or
  investment portfolio,
  leather bound   (+5 each)

CALCULATING THE SCORE

245 and above	**High-Net-Worth Intelligenzija**
185 – 245	**Conceptual Heaven**
100 – 185	**Freelance Purgatory**
50 – 100	**Normie Hellscape**
Below 50	**Rock-Bottom Basic**